American
Gastronomy

American Gastronomy

An illustrated portfolio
of recipes and culinary history

LOUIS SZATHMÁRY

Author of *The Chef's Secret Cook Book*

HENRY REGNERY COMPANY · CHICAGO

Jacket photograph of Louis Szathmáry by John L. Barton, Chicago

Contents

Foreword   7
American Foods   15
American Methods   21
American Cooks and Chefs   35
American Dishes   41
Converting Old Recipes for Today's Use   47
Notes   157
Metric Recipe Conversions   159
Cookbooks   177
Index to Recipes   181
Other Books by Louis Szathmáry   184

Foreword

Nearby as I write are almost six thousand cookbooks printed in the United States in my collection. More than five thousand of them were published since 1900; 270 date from the nineteenth century; a few were printed or handwritten in the 1700s.

Over the years I have read—or at least looked at—every page in all these volumes. Recently I have returned to many of them, checking carefully through dozens upon dozens of books on "American cookery" and "American foods" in an effort to define what we mean by the art or science of good American eating, or, in short, American gastronomy.

Not only could I find no definition, I failed to locate any explanation, opinion, or even statement about the nature of American gastronomy ... or American cuisine ... or American food.

So this vacuum in our culinary literature has become my challenge. After two decades of collecting and studying, I am at last able to present a definition of American gastronomy and to demonstrate what makes it different from any other in the world.

My research has extended far beyond my own collection of cookbooks. I have spent long days in some of the world's great libraries. I owe a special debt to the collection of Cornell University's School of Hotel Administration in Ithaca, New York. Profes-

A pictorial description of America, 1600s.

sor Margaret Spiney, Director of the Library, gave me valuable help and guidance, and directed me to many useful books.

I also am grateful to Professor Helen Recknegel, the editor of the *Cornell Quarterly,* and to Professor Matthew Bernatsky, who for many years held the Chair of Classic Cuisine at Cornell. Both were inspiring influences and guided me in worthwhile directions.

What, then, has this research produced? First, a definition of American gastronomy which I believe fairly represents what it involves:

The concept of American gastronomy includes those distinctively American methods, procedures, and utensils first used by the native Indians, and later by the colonists, pilgrims, and immigrants, in preparing for nourishment and enjoyment the native flora and fauna of the American continent, as well as the crops and animals subsequently domesticated by pre-Columbian Indians and American agriculturists.

As defined by Webster, "American" is an adjective describing anything "relating to or characteristic of the United States of America, its properties, culture, history, etc." According to the same source, "gastronomy" is "the art of good eating."

The key here is what I have found to be most characteristic of the people, culture, and history of the United States. For I believe the United States is the only kinetic country, the only truly mobile nation of Western civilization.

In Europe, population growth and the lack of geographical opportunities to expand or conquer without war have kept nations static through the ages. Over the last two thousand years the most populous European countries have become more and more settled in their ways. In order to survive, people in the Old World had to learn to live within their boundaries.

In the United States, on the other hand, Americans found they had to move constantly to survive. Colonists and immigrants learned to expand in order to find and reach their New World boundaries. This restlessness has continued to the present day and is now a deeply ingrained facet of the American character. It has made Americans a people on the go, a people who can never remain still in the sense that Europeans do.

One out of five American families, it is estimated, moves every year to another part of the country. The population is constantly moving, not only from region to region, from state to state, between East and West, North and South, but also from the farm lands to the cities, from the cities to the suburbs, from the suburbs

"Gentlemen's Supper," 1880s.

back to the cities, and even back to the countryside.

Not much happened to the wheel from the time of its invention in prehistoric times until the eighteenth century, but certainly more has happened to the wheel in the two-hundred-year history of the United States than in Europe in the thousands of years of its existence. True, the Roman Legions built excellent military highways in some regions of Europe; yet no part of the world has better road systems than the United States. Its ever-growing arteries link important cities and small communities throughout the continent.

More coaches, more railroads, more automobiles, and more airplanes have moved more Americans than any other people on the globe. Information is moved through more newspapers, periodicals, radio and television stations; more letters, telephone calls, and telegrams are exchanged than anywhere else in the world. To cite just one example, some eighty billion pieces of mail are sent and received in the United States each year—about half the total mail handled in all the rest of the world.

In a civilization that is always on the move, how could there possibly develop a regional cuisine in the European sense of the expression? If a new dish, like a new idea, were to originate in a particular region of this continent-sized country, who could expect it to remain in the same neighborhood for hundreds of years, as in Europe?

We can illustrate the contrast by taking Normandy, for example, a small northwestern section of France, similar in size to Massachusetts. For hundreds of years every housewife there has cooked with cream and calvados, which is a local apple brandy. Whatever she cooks, whether poultry, fish, veal, pork, or beef, she generally uses these two ingredients. But not one village, town, or city fifteen miles from the boundaries of Normandy would dream of serving a dish with cream and calvados as ingredients. Such insularity in the United States would be unthinkable.

Through innovations in transportation, the kinetic American has also made all the raw materials of food, which are seasonal in other parts of the world, available year-round.

Going a step further, food processing has become one of the largest industries in the United States. But one hundred years ago, when the country celebrated its centennial in Philadelphia, the food industry was not even mentioned among the "groups of manufacturers." The reason for its spectacular growth is the importance Americans place on time. Only a kinetic people can coin a phrase such as "Time is money." Where millions commute two and three hours a day to work, they have to figure their earnings to include their traveling time.

In a land where "time is money," bread is sold sliced; pancakes are frozen ready for the toaster; coffee is cooked ready to be dissolved in water; chicken is cut-up ready for the frying pan, and staples are pre-measured and pre-packed in convenient units.

American cookbooks reflect this same passion for ease of preparation. While the Old World has produced cookbooks since at least the first century (Apicius), an American author was the first to give precise amounts of ingredients, pre-measured not through some expensive and complicated device but with common, easily available, household utensils such as cups, tablespoons, and teaspoons.

This, then, is what American gastronomy is all about: native flora and fauna, prepared by American methods, and widely enjoyed by a fast-moving, highly mobile culture. To modify an old adage, we eat what we are. Our kinetic society has developed a cuisine perfectly suited to our demands for speed and quality. In the chapters that follow, we look more closely at the elements that make up American gastronomy.

NOTE
If you would prefer not to use this book during actual cooking, you may obtain a copy of the recipes for $2.00 by writing to Chef Louis Szathmáry, 2218 North Lincoln Avenue, Chicago, Illinois 60614.

"The Fourth of July in the Country," Harper's Weekly, *1867.*

American Foods

Whichever of the interpretations of the Europeans' discovery of America we choose to believe, one thing is certain: the explorers found an abundance of exotic, tasty, and easily obtainable foods. Unknown species of fish, strange-looking animals, fruits, vegetables, berries, and roots were everywhere. The Indians, hostile or friendly, had their own food staples which were given to (or taken away by) the hungry newcomers. These foods were sampled with curiosity.

The Indian tribes of Central and North America in the late fifteenth and early sixteenth centuries differed in many ways from one another, but most lived relatively well within their territories. We realize now that they had a reasonably advanced agriculture, through which they had skillfully converted many native plants into domesticated variations. Corn, different types of white and yellow potatoes, yams, cocoa, vanilla beans, tomatoes, and different members of the capcium (green pepper) family were sowed, watered, cultivated, and harvested. Wild animals were tamed and domesticated.

The first American settlers learned a great deal about food from the Indians, and taught them much, too. So did the colonists, and later, the European immigrants. In these early times, however, cookery was hardly a refined art; rather, it was a requisite for survival. Undoubtedly the difference between simple and festive meals in the early years was one of quantity more than of quality— a larger hunk of roast,[1] a larger bowl of soup,[2] a larger piece of cake.[3] These were the beginnings of memorable meals.

As the settlers began to organize their lives, cookbooks written and printed in England began arriving in the colonies. Only toward the end of the eighteenth century did some English publishers begin printing a different title page for editions to be shipped to the "New World." They also began to ship manuscripts to the colonies to be set in type and printed in Boston, New York, or Philadelphia. But still, the only "American" quality about these early cookbooks was the American designation in their titles.

Perhaps *American Cookery* by an "American Orphan" (1796) was the first American cookbook to include native plant names in its recipes. This first small American cookbook won popularity and was often reprinted, yet European offerings still predominated. But when the truly American cookbooks began to circulate, only the Bible was a better seller.

In the first decades of the nineteenth century, many clandestine publishers printed unauthorized editions of copyrighted books, and many authors and publishers never even bothered to copyright or to register their properties. Therefore we have no accurate sense of how many different books were written or published, and we cannot even guess how many copies of each were issued. Just one thing is certain: the better books remained in print for decades, and it was not unusual for a successful one to enjoy thirty or forty or more editions.[4]

How many of these books were "original," and how many were simply copied from previous or contemporary English cookbooks is difficult to say. The best way to determine their originality is to look for recipes for native American foods.

Which foods are native and which are not is extremely difficult to establish in some cases. Captain John Smith, in his book, *Smith's Virginia—Of Such Things which Are Naturally in Virginia, and How They Use Them,* writes:

Virginia doth afford many excellent vegetables, and living creatures. . . . The wood that is most common is

16

oak and walnut.... The acorns of one kind, whose
bark is more white than the other and somewhat
sweetish, which being boiled, at last affords a sweet
oil, that they keep in gourds to annoint their heads
and joints. The fruit they eat made in bread or otherwise. There is also some black walnut-tree.... Of
walnuts there is two or three kinds.... By the dwell-
ing of the savages are some great mulberry-trees....
In some parts were found some chestnuts, whose wild
fruit equal the best in France.... Plums there are of
three sorts. The red and white are like our hedge
plums, but the other, which they call putchamins,
grow as high as a palmeta.... It be not ripe, it will
draw a man's mouth awry, with much torment; but
when it is ripe, it is as delicious as an apricot. They
have cherries.... Of vines great abundance ... but
these bear few grapes. Except by the river and savage
habitations, where they are not overshadowed from
the sun, they are covered with fruit.... They have a
small fruit growing on little trees, husked like a
chestnut, but the fruit most like a very small acorn....

Was the Captain confused? Or was he describing vegetation
that had migrated, in the many strange ways of plant migration,
from other parts of the world to North America and into Virginia?
We cannot be sure, but we do know that certain vegetation and
animals are native to the Western hemisphere, especially the ones
that we know were domesticated by the pre-Columbian Indians:
potatoes, tomatoes, corn, cocoa, vanilla, to name some of the better
known, and sweet potatoes, yams, pumpkins, cranberries, wild rice,
okra, and lima beans, to name some others.

Captain Smith wrote about the animal kingdom as well:

...Of beasts the chief are deer, nothing differing from
ours.... Their partridges are little bigger than our
quails. Wild turkies are as big as our tame.[5]... In
winter there are great plenty of swans, cranes, grey
and white ... herons, geese, brants, duck, wigeon,
dotterell, oxies, parrots, and pigeons.... Of fish we
were best acquainted with sturgeon, grampus, porpus,
seals, stingrays ... brets, mullets, white salmons,
trouts, soals, plaice, herrings, coney-fish, rock-fish,

eels, lamprays, cat-fish, shads, perch of three sorts, crabs, shrimps, crevices, oysters, cockles and muscles. . . .

Some of these creatures are strange to us, some are familiar, but we know definitely there were American game and fish — Maine lobster, soft-shelled crab, whitefish, turkey, possum, and buffalo, among others.

The first cookbooks to utilize native edibles in abundance came from New England, New York, and Pennsylvania. Many recipes using native foods appear in Miss Leslie's *Directions for Cookery in its Various Branches,* Mrs. J. Chadwick's *Home Cookery: A Collection of Tried Receipts (both Foreign and Domestic),* E. Hutchinson's *The New Family Book; or Ladies' Indispensable Companion,* and Pierre Blot's *Hand-Book of Practical Cookery for Ladies and Professional Cooks.*

Blot's is the first among the cookbooks to address the professional cook as well as the homemaker and domestic servants. Many of the people who worked in inns, hotels, and restaurants considered cooking their vocation.

American gastronomy has always suffered a shortage of cooks, especially those who are native-born. From colonial times to the mid-twentieth century, most of the well-known cooks and chefs were foreign-born and emigrated to the United States as adults because of the need for their skills.

One of the first advertisements to appear in an American newspaper after the first president assumed his office was this one written personally by George Washington:

A COOK
Is wanted for the family of the President of the United States. No one need apply who is not perfect in the business, and can bring indubitable testimonials of sobriety, honesty and attention to the duties of the station.[6]

Significantly, the ad ran for a long time before a suitable applicant was found.

The Kamtchadal Indians smoking fish, old bookplate, unde

"Imported" cooks and chefs were highly esteemed and became "authorities" as soon as they learned to read and write English. Blot, the author of the *Hand-Book of Practical Cookery for Ladies and Professional Cooks,* was a Frenchman, and though his book mirrors his European training and skill, he soon became "Americanized." Reading his book, one can see that he addressed his words to Americans.

Without investigating the various motives that brought colonists, and later, immigrants to the New World, we can assume that they were more restless and dynamic than their countrymen who stayed behind. To decide on a long voyage to a strange new home is kinetic enough, but to settle and then move, and move again and then resettle, to expand and explore, is even more kinetic.

"Old Knickerbocker Tea-Table," magazine illustration, undated.

American Methods

Although they were called "settlers," and the places where they tried to establish roots were called "settlements," the early Americans were anything but settled in the European sense of the word. At first they tried to surround their habitats with the kinds of fortress-type enclosures they remembered from Europe. But they learned quickly and bitterly that walls built from logs offered little defense against Indian attacks. To survive meant to move, to be on the go, to disappear in the morning after covering the last traces of the campsite.

They also learned that to hunt, to fish, even to pick and collect vegetables, they had to be constantly on the move. So the first permanent settlements served mainly as points of departure and arrival for travelers. They were centers of distribution, places where messages could be left and picked up, where horses could be exchanged or purchased, guides and scouts hired, maps obtained, and provisions secured for the road, the river, or the ocean. The cities that were established embraced harbors, and for a long time no significant population settled in any location other than sheltered harbors, peninsulas, or on the banks of navigable rivers.

This was not, of course, an exclusively American phenomenon. Many of the world's great cities developed on seashores or

21

AMERICAN HOUSE.

BY

T. B. WINCHESTER.

BILL OF FARE.

Springfield, Oct 9th 1851.

Mock Turtle Soup.

FISH.

Boiled Bluefish

BOILED.

Chickens, Oyster Sauce.   Chickens and Pork.
Mutton, Caper Sauce.   Tongue.
        Corned Beef and Cabbage.
        Ham.

ENTREES.

ROAST.

Beef,   Veal,
Lamb,
Chickens,   Turkey.

PUDDINGS AND PASTRY.

Blanc Mange.

DESSERT.

Peaches

H. S. Taylor's Steam Presses, Sanford Street, and Massasoit Row.

Old menu from American House Restaurant, 1851.

river deltas, but an equal number developed because they were far away from road and water, because they were hidden in valleys or secure atop mountains.

Americans had no desire to be tucked away. If one would explore the reasons why railroads failed to fulfill the American Dream of Travel, he would find that to be track-bound is to be static. To stop at stations where one has nothing to do, where there is no need to get on or off, is a waste of time for the kinetic American.

The real American idea of moving from place to place is the automobile. To walk from one's bedroom into the kitchen, grab a slice of toast and a cup of coffee, continue from the kitchen right into the garage, enter the car, open the garage door with the touch of a finger, continue to listen to the same station on the car radio that one was listening to in bed, and finally to arrive at the garage, walk indoors, and ride the elevator up to one's office—this epitomizes the kinetic person's ideal in transportation.

Cooking methods and eating habits developed in America are the result of the same "on-the-go" style of living that has shaped motor transportation.

While the leavening described in the Old Testament is identical with San Francisco sourdough "starter," and while ovens have not changed basically since they were made of stone, American bread is now pre-sliced and pre-packaged. This innovation is the only dramatic change in the staple of Western civilization in the last five thousand years.

While several of the great European restaurants are still proud of their wood and coal cookstoves, the United States has the largest per capita share of gas, electric, and electronic ranges in the world. The stationary fireplace of the old colonial kitchen is no more. Today's modern grill, with long-lasting artificial coals and conveniently compact bottled gas, travels in the car trunk to the picnic grounds, or on a cross-country trip to the mountain ski lodge or the boat deck.

Cooking tasks that required manual labor and much time were made faster and easier by the invention of gadgets that eventually became our modern electrical appliances. The kinetic American has patented thousands of food-preparation gadgets—meat grinders, cherry pitters, apple corers and peelers, egg beaters, ice cream makers, butter churners, bread and meat slicers, juice pressers— that never existed before.

The Old World toaster was a double metal frame in which the hand-sliced bread was also turned by hand. The American toaster automatically receives the bread, toasts it to a pre-set color, then ejects it, hot and ready. Meanwhile, the electric beater beats the eggs; the grinder grinds the meat; the electric can opener turns and opens the can; the blender blends the fruit, and the percolator brews the coffee.

Energy for heat and power is not carried on a person's back from the cellar in the form of coal; it runs through gas pipes or electric wires to every necessary point in the kitchen. Even the kitchen refuse is ground to a pulp and flushed down the sink drain.

American methods enable the homemaker to concentrate on the most important tasks in food preparation, without having to do chores on the farm, in the warehouse, at the food-processing plant, or in the supermarket. Take something as simple as the peanut. In earlier days the raw peanut had to be roasted and salted at home, then shelled, chopped, and ground to be made into peanut butter. First, roasting and salting was industrialized, then the shelling. After that, the grocery set up large grinders in the store. Today, peanut butter arrives ready to be spread.

Bacon, ham, cold cuts, popcorn, cookies, and many other staples underwent a change in the United States, after centuries of unchanging preparation in European kitchens. Beans and rice now come pre-cooked; chicken is cut into portions; pork loins are sliced into chops, and meat is ground—and also sometimes spiced, formed into patties, and even pre-cooked.

None of these methods remained unique to a single region of the country, or to a single ethnic or social group. Whenever methods were invented, improved, or simplified, they spread quickly throughout the United States, giving every American the chance to choose those most suitable to him.

Some of these methods were short-lived (pressure cooking is a good example). Others grew from small regional or ethnic beginnings into national successes. Barbecuing started as a local custom in Atlanta after the Civil War, and it spread from the Golden Gate Bridge to Martha's Vineyard.

Chow mein and chop suey were concocted in San Francisco's Chinatown, and became popular not only in the United States but in other parts of the world—just as the great "Italian delicacy" invented in New York, the "authentic, original, and only" pizza pie![7]

On the first American printed menu, at Delmonico's in New

Bread-slicing machine, an American invention.

York about 1836, one of the most expensive dishes—something very new and very New Yorkish—was "Hamburg Steak." An imported delicacy? Checking through German food encyclopedias, food dictionaries, and gastronomic handbooks, one can find several entries from Hamburg. In my library I have three editions of the *Universal Lexikon der Kochkunst,* the oldest one having been printed in 1881, and under the heading "Hamburg," one finds eel soup, coffee cake, dumplings, ham, mayonnaise, and smoked meat—but no hamburger as we know it.

In *Das Hauswesen,* printed in 1883, one of the best and most comprehensive German cookbooks of its time, only cheesecake is listed as being from Hamburg; and the Blueher's *Rechtschreibung,* a French, German, and English dictionary of food, names a dozen dishes from Hamburg—but not one we know as hamburger. The book contains a large selection of European menus, among them several from Hamburg, but again, there is no trace of what we call hamburger.

The well-known cookbook author, Jules Gouffe, whose *Die Feine Kuche* (1872) contains about twenty pages of beef dishes, lists nothing similar to hamburger.

On the other hand, the Delmonico's menu has "Hamburg Steak" on it—well before any other traceable source mentioned the city of Hamburg in connection with a ground beef dish.

Looking again at Blueher's *Rechtschreibung,* one finds a recipe for beefsteak in which he mentions that chopped beefsteak in America is called Hamburg Steak. This information, dated from 1899 and found in a German book, would seem to prove that the dish was indeed named and probably originated in the United States. The reasons behind the creation of hamburger make a fascinating culinary detective story as well as a perfect illustration of how a food develops out of social conditions.

The first Americans were Englishmen, but by the 1830s the New World had become a growing attraction for Europeans weary of wars, famine, and hopelessness. As they decided to leave, Western and Middle Europeans gravitated toward the most important mainland port of Europe—Hamburg. This was where Bavarians, Saxons, Austro-Hungarians, Belgians, Swiss, Dutch, and Prussians waved goodbye to the old continent and embarked for the new.

Arriving in the New World, especially in the late 1820s and early 1830s, skilled, young European craftsmen immediately secured jobs and began to earn relatively good wages. In American restaurants they looked, of course, for something familiar from their homelands. Most of the foods they found were of Anglo-Saxon origin and were as strange to them as native American dishes. But the name *Hamburg* and the memory of the German Hackbraten—things that had nothing whatsoever to do with the American hamburger—looked familiar, and lured them into restaurants.

Domestic cookbooks, even the very best ones, in the middle and later nineteenth century, have no recipe for hamburger—except for cookbooks written by professional chefs working in large New York restaurants. The only domestic cookbook of the time with a dish named "hamburger steak" (not hamburger as we know it) is the early edition of Mrs. Lincoln's *Boston Cook Book.*

The recipe that most closely resembles what we know today as an American hamburger is in the excellent book by Allessandro Filippini, *The Table,* published in 1890, after the author had worked as head chef at Delmonico's for twelve years. Filippini's recipe calls for running a steak through a Salisbury grinder. This, too, indicates that the hamburger was American in origin, for the Germans certainly would not have developed a dish which relied upon a British invention.

Clearly, American culinary genius invented hamburger. From gastronomical, culinary, and nutritional points of view, it is the most characteristic of American dishes. It can be as good or bad as can be a truffled breast of pheasant under glass, depending on how it is prepared.

To produce a delicious hamburger, one needs know-how and proper equipment, besides good ingredients. A well-regulated source of heat is required, with quick heat recovery and a wide range—very high heat is required for the meat and constant medium heat for the bun. Obviously a refrigerator and freezer are useful, as are, for restaurants, a well-controlled meat grinder, a good automatic vegetable slicer, and an automatic rotating bake oven. In the end, it is easier for a French chef with a knife and an open fire to create a culinary masterpiece than it is for him to produce a perfect hamburger. This is what makes the hamburger distinctively American.

Many other dishes we enjoy today, whatever their origins, have become authentically American because of American methods and equipment. To name a few: the unsurpassed and inimitable

American ingenuity created new machines for kitchen use: from top left, stove, vertical ice-cream freezer from cornstarch ad, and newfangled gas stove.

American ice cream, the perfect beef steak, potato chips, peanut butter, and maple syrup. Each of these foods owes its success to a method of preparation.

The perfect ice cream, for example, demanded a process that would combine expensive, high-quality raw ingredients into a relatively inexpensive product conveniently available to all Americans.

The perfect steak called for a feeding method that would develop cattle into "choice" or "prime" beef of a quality which has never been matched for eating enjoyment by any other beef anywhere in the world.

To perfect the potato chip, an intricate production and packaging technology had to be worked out to make this brittle, fragrant, and very perishable product readily available—and fresh—on grocery shelves all over the country.

Actually, the methods unique to American gastronomy are not only those of food preparation. The whole process begins with soil conservation, seed and stock selection, and agricultural methods. In addition, because of the country's geographic scope, transportation, warehousing, marketing, selling, advertising, merchandising, and packaging all must function on a highly efficient level. Nothing new, nothing exciting can be kept local or regional for very long. Even in the first half of the nineteenth century, the New England housewife had access to merchandise from all over the United States and the world.

In Boston to cook from Miss Leslie's book, *Directions for Cookery in Its Various Branches* (1848), one of the great and influential household manuals of the time, one needed to have in the larder or readily available at the nearby grocery: almonds, anchovies, anise, apricots, arrowroot, artichokes, asparagus, barley, beans, beer, biscuits, bitters, bran, buckwheat, butter, capers, cayenne pepper, chestnuts, chili, chocolate, cocoa, currants. The list goes on to include hundreds of articles that today's homemaker would not begin to know where to find. Who today would know where to get elder flower wine, fox grapes, or fresh ginger?

Just after the Civil War, Pierre Blot, in New York, offers recipes for "Ladies and Professional Cooks." In his section on "Game Cookery," he suggests ways to prepare wild ducks, geese, pigeon, wild turkey, bear, buffalo, blackbird, bobolinks, reed birds, rice birds, lapwings, meadowlarks, plovers, rails, robins, snipes, thrushes, woodcocks, woodpeckers, yellow birds, opossum, otter, racoon, skunk, fox, woodchuck, squirrel, elk, and deer. Of course,

Hotel Astor, Times Square, New York. The kitchen, 231 feet long

all such game had to arrive in New York fresh, so the author provides a short, informative section on transportation, storage, and freezing.

American techniques of preserving food are remarkably advanced and different from other countries of the Western world. These basic differences arise, again, from the kinetic nature of Americans. American foods are preserved in relatively small and easy to transport units as compared with those in the Old World. The "static" European preserved four hundred pounds of cabbage and made a barrel of sauerkraut. The American homemaker puts her kraut in small jars or buys it at the supermarket. When families are constantly moving, when people are always on the move, slaughtered cattle are not packed into large barrels of cured meat; they are butchered into small cuts.

In general, Americans have seized every opportunity to condense and reduce. Vanilla, the American flavoring and spicing

agent, is the fruit of the vanilla orchid, domesticated by the pre-Columbian Indians. In the United States it is sold as concentrated extract. In Europe it is sold in the bulkier form of vanilla sugar.

There is nothing new about food vendors bringing food to the people, instead of people going to the store. Still, static and kinetic civilizations differ greatly in their approaches to this custom. The Italian ice-cream vendor fills his ice-packed cart and moves it to an area where there is a large concentration of people—all prospective customers. There he remains until all his goods are sold. The American vendor stays on the move, and seeks out customers in places where it might not even be profitable to set up a food stand.

Likewise in catering. In middle Europe from the Near East to England, persons with great skill in cooking moved from home to home, from village to village, from castle to castle, cooking meals for weddings, birthdays, patron saint days, and similar occasions. Everything they prepared, and everything they prepared it in and

31

with, belonged to the family or the community. The idea that the caterer brings not only his skill but also the food and the equipment—chairs, tables, tableware—is an American idea. It has spread from the United States back to the Old World, where it is just starting to gain popularity.

Of all the methods of preparing food, the most significant and most American is what the whole world calls, for some strange reason, the French stove. A Connecticut-born-and-reared Yankee, Benjamin Thompson, conceived the brilliant idea of surrounding a metal box with hot air. When it is horizontal, it can be used for baking. A door on the front and a small vent regulate the amount of heat retained. When it is vertical, it can be used for boiling; the opening becomes a lid, and the fire itself is generated in a special compartment above which a series of rings regulate the heat.

The French ridiculed Thompson and wanted nothing to do with the invention, so he took it to Bavaria, where the king used the stove in feeding the army and the poor. He knighted Thompson and gave him the title of Count Rumford.

This invention and the Franklin stove, designed by Benjamin Franklin, have provided the basic methods of regulating heat for cooking, baking, frying, grilling, broiling, roasting, simmering, or sautéing.

Now the first major advance in cookery since Count Rumford's invention of the French stove is again American—the electronic oven. In conventional cooking, the heat penetrates the surface of the food first, and then moves through it toward the center. In electronic cooking, heat is generated first in the center of the food, and from there spreads toward the surface. This method is not yet perfected, just as canning of food was not perfected when Nicholas Alpert invented it to help feed Napoleon's army.

While canning was definitely a European invention, its widest application and best methods were developed in the United States. Canning means to cook on an assembly line, and for some foods it is still the best method of preparation and preservation. Certain canned foods have become *sui generi,* such as sardines, applesauce, and catsup. The ingredients and the method have combined to become a new product, leaving the original ingredients without the method of secondary importance.

If you say sardines, you think of canned sardines. If you do not, then you must add the word *fresh* in order to be understood. With catsup, applesauce, and many other canned or bottled foods, the adjective *homemade* or *fresh* must be added to differentiate them from their usual form.

As commercial canned and preserved foods improved and their usage spread, American cookbooks devoted less and less space to pickling and other home methods of preserving. The thirty-first edition of Miss Leslie's *Directions for Cookery in Its Various Branches* contains eighteen pages on preserving. Mrs. Chadwick's *Home Cookery,* published in 1853, contains eleven pages on jellies and preserves and another five pages on pickles. As late as 1875, *The Presbyterian Cook Book,* one of the early community cookbooks, compiled by the Ladies of the First Presbyterian Church of Dayton, Ohio, includes many pages on catsups—tomato mustard, cucumber, walnut, mushroom, wild plum, gooseberry, currant, grape; ten pages on pickles and relishes; and seven pages on canned fruits and vegetables.

But as the United States moved into the twentieth century, very few such recipes could still be found in American cookbooks. The catsups, relishes, and home-canned items that remained were included largely for their nostalgic curiosity.

Of course, every state and county fair still gives prizes for home canning, preserving, and pickling. A few years ago, newspapers told the story of a California state fair at which the winner of the gold medal for canned peaches, canned pears, canned vegetables, corn relish, sweet pickles, gherkins, and several other categories turned out to be a newspaperman who later confessed that all the items he had entered were the products of a canning factory. He had carefully transferred the foods into home-canning jars and hand-labeled them. What's more, all the items had been purchased in cut-rate grocery stores!

The point here is that hardly any home canner or home preserver, even the very best, can compete with the equipment, know-how, and methods of the American food manufacturer.

American Cooks and Chefs

Why were good professional chefs and cooks so scarce in the early United States? First, native Americans rarely chose the profession because so many other possibilities were available to them. Second, the first cooks and chefs to work here were immigrants who kept the secrets of their trade very much to themselves. Great hotels and restaurants customarily brought their chefs from Europe, especially France, Switzerland Germany, Austria, and Italy. In turn, the chefs brought with them their own crews, or they would choose their kitchen help from among their own national groups.

In households the situation was little different. We forget that domestic help was not always a luxury for the American housewife. Such help came basically from two groups—newly arrived immigrants and American blacks. As a consequence, both groups very noticeably have influenced the core of American cuisine.

A British traveler who visited Virginia in the early nineteenth century wrote of his dining experience in the modest cabin of a slave family, to which he had been invited for a meal:

> ... Whilst my lunch was in preparation, I employed myself in surveying the room. The chimney occupied one entire end of the house; that is to say, was about fifteen feet in width. In the middle of this was the fire, leaving room on either side for seats. Opposite to each were two small windows, or "light-holes" as the negroes sometimes call them, each having a shelf beneath it. The two corners most remote from the fireplace were occupied, one by a little table with a

small triangular deal cupboard nailed above it to the wall—the other by a homminy-mortar. Behind the door a very small shelf supported the good man's razors, etc.; and just above this depended from a nail, a very irregular polygon of looking-glass, fitted into a piece of pine bark by way of frame. Near the fire stood, on one side, a spinning-wheel, and on the other, a bedstead and bed. A short ladder in one corner terminated at a square hole in the ceiling, and formed a communication with the loft, which is used as a storeroom for broom-corn, shuck-mats, etc. It may be necessary to explain that "shuck" is a name here given to the husk that envelopes the ear of the Indian corn, and of which the negroes make mats, chair-bottoms, and even horse-collars, for sale. High on the wall hung some half dozen dry, inflated bladders, and many festoons of capsicum. . . .A little cross-legged table was put before me, upon which were spread fried eggs, sweet potatoes roasted in hot ashes, bread baked upon a hoe* and a plate of honey. I found no difficulty in doing justice to this display of hospitality. . . .[1]

Plain ingredients, inventive methods, primitive utensils—but together, they turned simple foods into handsome meals.

Black people have been highly regarded for their culinary skills throughout American history. Apparently no one could please George Washington's palate (a palate particularly difficult to please, associated as it was with teeth carved from wood, later whale bone and ivory) except a black cook named Hannibal. Hannibal's services were so much in demand that he spent much of his time traveling between home and capital. We know from Washington's correspondence that no matter which place he was, he wanted Hannibal's cuisine.

Throughout the early twentieth century, even into the late 1930s, some food companies showed a black chef in their advertising. Many products became successful partly because they relied on advertising and promotion that showed a black woman cook as the originator or developer of the product. Aunt Jemima became an in-

*A kind of griddle.

stitution—and an unsurpassed moneymaker—as the result of an advertising illustration.

Meanwhile, only a few chefs—in the international usage of the word—became part of the American culinary legend. Oscar of the Waldorf, Philippe of Delmonico's, and the incomparable Rector were once admired in households from coast to coast, just as today almost every American knows the names of James Beard, Julia Child, and Graham Kerr (the Galloping Gourmet). But from the beginning, the real hero of American cuisine has been "Mrs. American Homemaker." A look at American cookbooks tells why.

On the list of fifteen recommended books (comprising twenty-seven American cookbooks) listed at the end of this book, there is among the authors only one professional chef, Pierre Blot. The list includes eleven women known by name, and the remaining books were written, edited, or compiled by groups of homemakers. This is typically American. Among early European cookbooks, hardly any are written by homemakers. Of course, the American example slowly spread back to the Old World, and in the twentieth century we find more or less successful attempts to copy this American custom in many countries.

In the United States the study of home economics was from the beginning a women's pursuit, and it became the first field of endeavor in which women outnumbered men. The role of women has been significant not only with regard to food itself but also in many fields related to food. These include kitchen design and the design and use of cooking vessels, utensils, stoves and ranges, table linens, serving dishes, decorations, silver, and glassware.

The early American table was neither sophisticated nor elegant, but it had a simple beauty about it. Although most of the table settings in colonial times were made of wood or locally fired clay, early settlers also brought with them some pewter and other metal pieces, and in some cases stoneware, china, and glass. Pewter, an alloy of lead and tin, was the principal metal, and every small colonial town had a pewtersmith who could repair, remelt, or recast pewter. This is probably why so few early American pieces have survived—when they were bent, scratched, or otherwise damaged, they were simply reworked into new pieces.

The inexpensive but handsome pottery, the well-designed and carefully carved wooden pieces, and the metallic glow of the pewter set a pretty table. As a centerpiece, almost every woman had a treasured piece of china, glass, or other favorite she had brought from the Old World.

Later, American tableware manufacturers and importers changed this picture. By the time of the *Kansas Home Cook Book,* published in Leavenworth in 1886, we read:

> ... In every department of home-life great attention is now given to internal decoration, and the dining-room receives its full share of thought and study. Fortunately, beautiful and charming table-adornments are now within the reach of persons of very moderate means. Upon the shelves of our china-stores may be found handsome imitations of highly-colored costly wares, from which a few selections, interspersed among the pure white china, will greatly enliven the general effect of a table set in the ordinary colorless ware.... [2]

But the kitchen was where the most significant difference between American and European homes appeared. Even in France, where food is seemingly more important than in other European countries, the kitchen is dark, hidden, uncomfortable, and totally utilitarian. But in the American home the kitchen is the home-maker's sanctuary, a center of activities, and the focal point of family life. The food is not only prepared but in many cases is eaten in the kitchen. Here neighbors visit and business is conducted. The kitchen is designed to be sunny, well lighted, easily accessible, and roomy.

The early American kitchen, with its single knife, several wooden spoons, two or three wooden mixing bowls, and pails for drinking and cooking water, became more and more a collection of gadgets, utensils, and tools for the convenience of the American homemaker. The single kitchen knife was soon joined by the vegetable peeler, lemon slicer, food chopper, meat grinder, cheese grater, cherry pitter, apple corer, grapefruit segmenter, clam opener, roast beef slicer, poultry scissors, cheese cutter, butter knife, sandwich spreader, fish knife, fruit knife, and ice cream scoop—all basic variations of the knife, since all had blades designed to do specialized tasks in the kitchen. Garlic presses, lemon and orange squeezers, potato mashers, can openers, knife

A state dinner at the White House.

"New York City. A Free Lesson to Young Housekeepers—A Character Scene on a Fashionable Avenue," Frank Leslie's Illustrated Newspaper, *1882.*

sharpeners, bottle openers, corkscrews, meat thermometers, electric blenders, electric toasters, and thousands of other gadgets come and go. There was a time when no kitchen was without an assortment of sieves or strainers for tea, but with the advent of the tea bag they have all gone the way of the coffee mill and the special cutting frame for French fries.

American Dishes

Because the origin of so many recipes and dishes is legend and hearsay more than documented fact, it is difficult to pinpoint precisely where and how a dish first evolved, or when it was served for the first time. Nevertheless, it is easy to prove that many dishes now served throughout the world originated in the United States and then spread to other parts of the globe.

Corn or maize is an American grain, and in addition to cornflakes, many other forms of this important food are truly American—corn cakes, hushpuppies, cornbread, fried corn mush, corn chowder, and Indian pudding, to name just a few. Any dish that uses a coating of cornflakes instead of breading—as in oven-baked chicken—must be considered as American as ham and eggs, another old favorite which resulted from having only one frying pan on a covered wagon crossing the prairies. Born of necessity, ham and eggs became a culinary delight highly regarded throughout the world.

Few realize that the pancake, as we know it, is a truly American dish, still unknown in some parts of the world. Every civilization has mixed ground seeds with liquids, and then baked, cooked, or fried the mixture in rounded portions. It is the fastest and easiest way to turn the raw flour mixture into an edible dish. But the result of mixing baking powder, eggs, and milk into corn or wheat flour, or into a mixture of the two, without adding sugar; cooking it; and then, serving it with another native American product, maple or corn syrup, is uniquely American.

The American pancake bears little resemblance to the round, thin piece of pan-cooked dough that the French call crêpes; the

The Annual Dinner of the New York Yacht Club, 1891.

Hungarians, palacsinta; and almost every other European language calls something different. Inexpert food editors and translators, translate the American pancake into crêpes, omelet, and who knows what else, but they are incorrect. (The best-known version of the European dessert crêpe is the world famous Crêpes Suzette, but very few know that it was invented by accident and first served by its inventor, Henri Charpentier, during his younger days as an apprentice chef in France. The dish acquired its reputation in New York and later in Chicago, where Charpentier, one of the great chefs of this century, worked most of his life serving his Crêpes Suzette to gourmets, gourmands, socialites, and travelers from the world over.)

The American pancake is served as a wholesome breakfast or luncheon dish. Crêpes and their like are always served either sweet, as a dessert, or with a savory filling as an appetizer or light main course.

It is common knowledge that the potato had its origin in the fields around the dwellings of pre-Columbian Indians. Less well known is the fact that mashed potatoes, a mixture of potatoes, milk, and butter or other shortening, is peculiarly American. One of the rarest cookbooks, *Ein Neu Kochbuch,* by Marx Rumpolt (1587), contains the first recipe for cooking potatoes. The recipe, of pre-Columbian Indian origin, is titled *Erdtepffel,* which derives from the earliest German word for potato (the German equivalent of the French *pommes de terre* and later called *Kartoffel*). Apparently the recipe was brought back by Spanish sailors from the second voyage of Columbus, and presented by Queen Isabella of Spain to other rulers and important churchmen, along with a few potatoes, sweet potatoes, and yams. Translated, the recipe reads: "Peel and chop it small, soak it in water and press it out through a cheesecloth. Chop it even finer, and first simmer it through with minced fat, then add milk, mix it through, and let it simmer this way. It will be good and tasty."[1]

The renowned potato chip was created at a famous resort hotel in Saratoga Springs. Parker House rolls were first made in Boston, at the venerable Parker House Hotel, and a New England chef of British origin, a Mr. Newburg, created Shrimp Newburg in the 1860s. He was the first to make a sauce in which paprika and sherry were combined for a unique taste.

Menus all over the world refer to Eggs Benedict by such names as Eggs Benedictine or Eggs Benedictus, assuming the dish has

A Lunch Room,
magazine illustration, 1875.

something to do with the French order of monks. Actually this dish, consisting of an English muffin (also an American food) and a slice of Canadian bacon, covered with a poached egg, hollandaise sauce, and a slice of truffle (originally a California black olive), was ordered by its inventor, a commercial traveler named Benedict, at Diamond Jim's in New York.

Two strictly American salads have conquered the culinary world. One is the Waldorf Salad which combines apples, celery, and walnuts with mayonnaise, and was created at the Waldorf Hotel in New York. The other is Caesar Salad, the brainchild of a restaurant owner on the American side of the Mexican border in Tijuana, where his family still owns and operates the restaurant he founded.

The word *steak* appears in some early English cookbooks, but what the world today calls *beefsteak* or *steak* is a 100 per cent original American creation—"often imitated, never duplicated" anywhere in the world. The very last part of its preparation, the broiling, makes the American steak what it is, but the process starts much earlier. It is possible because of American mobility. Not only were beef animals moved unbelievable distances for grazing, but bulls were moved for breeding purposes to distant ranches by railroad, truck, and later airplane for more than a century. Now, artificial insemination has made it possible for whole herds in faraway places to be fertilized by the same male to produce uniform-quality offspring. Beef animals are scientifically selected, bred, fed and reared. After scientific aging, the meat becomes the unsurpassed American steak.

Yankee pot roast and what the world knows today as beef stew are entirely American in origin as well, and their internationally accepted recipes are also American.

The origin of Maine lobster is obvious, but few persons realize that certain other dishes made from crustaceans are also native American. Throughout the world a delightful shrimp creation is known and savored as Shrimp de Jonghe. Raw shrimp are gently sautéed in butter and garlic, then baked with herbs and buttered crumbs in a coquille shell. This is the invention of a famous Dutch chef, who created it while working at Jacques Restaurant in Chicago. Shrimp creole, shrimp remoulade, oysters Rockefeller, and she-crab soup are also American dishes.

An American fish that we now consider a staple once created a sensation on the finest dining tables of Europe. The Chicago Art Institute has a lithographed handwritten menu by artist Henri de Toulouse-Lautrec, which he used in his own household when he invited guests. Its *pièce de résistance* is "Lake Trout from Lake Michigan." The fish were shipped live in a tank by railroad and ship from Chicago to Paris before the turn of the century.

Converting Old Recipes for Today's Use

The recipes that follow are drawn from classic American cookbooks. They have been selected from twenty-six books, adapted for modern-day cookery, and then tested several times to be sure they could be easily reproduced without losing their authenticity. Throughout the experimental work, procedures were developed that will enable a homemaker to convert almost any recipe in any American cookbook into usable form. Allowances have been made for the fact that staple ingredients such as salt, flour, shortening, and sugar, as well as meat, poultry, fruits, and vegetables, have gone through considerable changes in processing and packaging in the years since the old books were first published.

Many of the authors of these books assumed that their readers were experienced cooks. Consequently, methods were only sketchily described, and cooking times and temperatures were either omitted or vague (hot, medium, until done, and so forth). These omissions have been clarified. Here are some suggestions that will be especially helpful in converting old recipes from other books:

(1) Read the recipe at least twice.
(2) Make a list of the ingredients and utensils needed.
(3) Make sure you have all the ingredients and utensils on

hand, or easily obtainable. You may have to consider different terminology in order to find needed raw materials. For instance, some recipes in old cookbooks require "mature corn" or "dry whole corn"—items that are no longer called by their original names. No one in food markets will know what you want. But almost all stores carry "mature corn" for making popcorn. If you ask for corn for popping you will have no difficulty, and then you can boil, bake, or sauté it as a recipe requires.

Many other ingredients are not available in groceries anymore, even though they used to be staples. But many of them may be obtained in health or natural food stores. Some ingredients may be available in stores catering to ethnic groups. Chilis and peppers, corn flour and cornmeal may be available in groceries in Latin neighborhoods, just as certain kinds of noodles and unusual spices and herbs may be available only in Oriental neighborhood shops.

(4) After you have assembled all the ingredients, be careful to recognize changes in them since the book was written or the recipe invented.

For example, flour used to contain a higher percentage of moisture. Therefore, after sifting and measuring the amount of flour required, it is advisable to remove ½ tablespoon of flour from each cup required in an old recipe. You can always replace it if, during preparation, the dough seems looser than it should be.

Sugar now is cleaner, sweeter, and has a stronger concentration of pure crystals, so it is advisable to start with less than an old recipe calls for.

Milk today is homogenized, and it has a much higher fat content. Therefore, two tablespoonsful per cup of milk should be replaced by water.

When cream is listed as an ingredient in a recipe, half-and-half, medium cream, or light cream will serve in place of heavy or whipping cream. Heavy cream should be used only when a recipe explicitly requires it or to make whipped cream.

Eggs today are larger. Extra-large eggs did not exist until thirty or forty years ago. As a rule, when preparing something from an older recipe, medium-sized eggs will do, or the number of eggs can be cut down—for each six eggs required, five large or extra-large will do. Because egg white tends to harden doughs, be especially careful to adjust the amount in recipes calling for them.

When whipping cream or beating egg whites with an electric beater, the volume will be greater more quickly than with a hand beater. Overbeating also occurs much more easily with an electric beater. So when the amount of whipped cream or beaten egg whites is given, you can expect to achieve greater volume with an electric beater and may want to reduce the amount of egg whites accordingly. Because whipped cream is usually not used in cooking proper, it will not do much harm to have more or less than the exact amount required, but it is different with egg whites—too much whipped egg whites can affect texture and cooking time.

Butter and shortening are more uniform today, and they contain more fat and less liquid. Many old recipes require that butter be clarified, which is unnecessary today. Lard has a much higher frying efficiency than other shortenings; you can usually use less lard to fry more food at a higher temperature than with other shortenings. Therefore, foods fried correctly in lard will have more color on the outside and less saturation on the inside. A mixture of lard and butter, oil and butter, or oil and lard is always better for frying, sautéing, or braising than using one type of shortening alone. If the frying is done in a processed shortening, or in lard, but a butter flavor is desired, toss the fried food with a small amount of fresh, room-temperature butter for a surprisingly delightful butter flavor.

Not only in frying, but also in baking, the type of shortening makes a great difference. Lard goes a longer way than butter; if margarine is used, the amount should be considerably greater than with other shortenings. As a general rule, if a dough made from one pound of sifted flour requires one cup of lard in the recipe, then one cup plus two tablespoons of butter, or one cup plus four tablespoons of margarine will provide the same amount of "shortening" in the dough. (Most recipes for pie dough in old cookbooks do require lard, and many homemakers who normally would not use lard as a shortening in cooking will make their pie dough with lard.)

Baking powder and baking soda have been greatly improved. Today's baking powder is more effective and more reliable than it used to be. Therefore a smaller amount usually will do. Many cookbooks use two ingredients—baking powder and baking soda—interchangeably, but recipes that call for baking soda should be made with any of the known brands of bicarbonate of soda as a leavening agent, to retain their original characteristics.

Fresh yeast or cake yeast is, as a rule, available most places. If a store carries it, it will most likely be found in a refrigerated display case, or with ready-to-bake doughs. But today's excellent dry yeast, which comes in powder form and is sold in single-unit envelopes, is just as good. It is important to note the date on the envelope, because dry yeast has a limited shelf life. Unsuccessful baked goods often are a result of overaged yeast. It is also important not to use a liquid that is too hot or too cold to activate the yeast, because it destroys the yeast's power to raise the dough.

No other ingredient has experienced so dramatic a change as meat. Beef is more tender, better marbled, and tastier than ever before. Complaints about beef not being as tasty as it used to be may arise from the fact that only a few cuts are still used. In the past almost nothing was ground, and cuts now forgotten or unknown were made into tasty dishes by braising, baking, simmering, and other slow-cooking processes. Today, except for roast beef and pot roast, everything is grilled, broiled, or cooked quickly. Only the most tender—and least tasty—cuts are suitable for this method.

Whatever the reason, cooking times specified in old cookbooks are usually too long, and cooking temperatures are too high. Most experts today agree that roasting should be done in a 350-degree oven. The internal temperature for rare to medium-rare roast beef should not be more than 110 degrees when removed from the oven; for medium, 140 degrees; and for well-done, 160 degrees. Beef should not be boiled, even if the recipe calls for "boiling." Simmering, which means keeping the liquid just below 212 degrees, is the ideal temperature. One old rule does remain valid today: if the broth is important, the meat should be put into cold water in a cold pot, and the water and the meat slowly heated together. If the meat itself is important, it will be tastier if it is immersed in boiling liquid.

The taste of pork has declined somewhat, but the quality, the ratio of meat versus fat, the chewiness, and the digestibility are improved. Many persons think pork is more fattening than beef, and they avoid recipes requiring pork. But this assumption is unfounded. In most cases the fat is completely removed, because the pork has no marbling except in certain parts of the shoulder. A trimmed pork chop has fewer calories and less saturated fat than a beef steak of the same weight.

In general pork should be cooked, baked, or roasted for shorter periods of time than suggested by cookbooks of even ten years ago. For well-done pork, an internal temperature of 160 degrees is adequate. Most cookbooks still recommend 180 degrees, which is really unnecessary.

THE WEBSTER PIG.

Among Daniel Webster's many well-known interests was the improvement of food, especially animal food. The subject of this engraving, dated 1854, is a Chinese pig imported by Webster from Portugal. Inopportunely, it arrived on the day of Webster's death, so the family gave the pig to a Mr. Kimball, who bred it. It is one of the forebears of today's American pig.

Today's lamb is more tender and carefully fed, and the ratio of bone to meat is more favorable than it was years ago. Cooking times can be shorter.

The poultry industry has developed in great leaps. Frying and roasting chickens have become more uniform, plumper, and more tender than their ancestors. Cooking times should therefore be much shorter, except for simmering or stewing, which still requires several hours of cooking before the gelatinous substance on the joints of the bones and in the skin turns into a water-soluble substance and becomes part of the cooking liquid. The recent scientific work of Dr. Charles Rogers and others proves beyond a doubt that poultry flavor comes from the skin and the joints. People recognize the flavor of poultry only when a food has been prepared with the skin.

Domestic animals on a New England farm, an original etching, 1832.

Experience with fish and seafood has shown that old cook-books, almost without exception, suggest too long a cooking time and too high a temperature. Fish should be cooked only until it becomes firm—usually when the internal temperature at the thickest part reaches 130 to 140 degrees. If the filets are thin and are to be pan-fried, sautéed, or baked in an oven-proof serving dish or casserole, fifteen to twenty minutes is usually enough.

Shrimp, lobster, lobster tails, and other crustaceans should also be cooked for a much shorter time than is usually suggested. If cooked in the shell, the food is usually done when the shell turns pink or red. In the case of larger lobsters, an additional five minutes is sufficient in most cases.

Changes in the growing and harvesting of potatoes, carrots, onions, and other vegetables have not had a significant effect on the

The old West Washington food market, New York City, 1871.

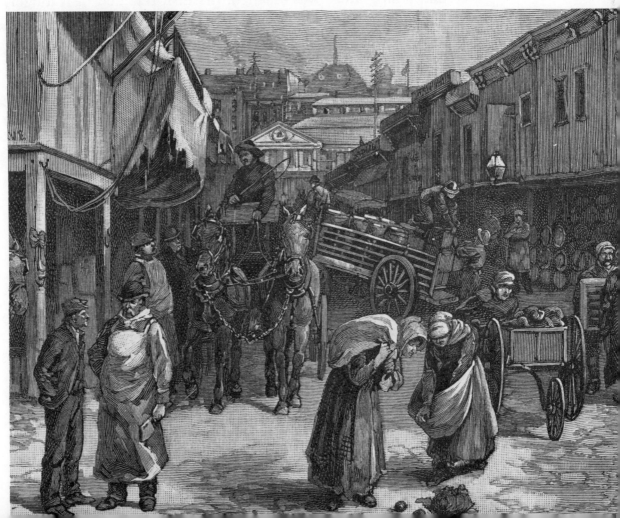

cooking process. In many old recipes requiring fresh vegetables, it is easy to substitute frozen or, in certain cases, canned vegetables. Again, a general rule is that shorter cooking times are advisable, and, to bring out the flavor, a very small amount of sugar should be added with the salt—not more than ½ teaspoon of sugar for a 12-ounce package of frozen vegetables. It will just heighten and balance the flavor, not sweeten the dish.

Tools and utensils have changed even more than ingredients since the days of old cookbooks. Hand beaters and copper bowls are very much a part of the past. Almost every household now has a mechanical egg beater, either hand or electric, so beating times are much shorter. Again be careful not to overbeat.

Meat grinders are more efficient and easier to handle.

Cookware itself can be crucial to results, and one must be careful when substituting new utensils for old ones. Many old puddings, soufflés, and molded cakes were baked or cooked in thick, glazed ceramic dishes and molds. Heat penetrated slowly, and once a certain temperature was reached, the dish retained heat longer, with a much slower heat loss through temperature change. Today, metal utensils in a pre-heated oven heat much faster than ceramic, and this sometimes cuts down on the cooking time required. On the other hand, opening and closing an oven door while a pudding or soufflé is baking affects the temperature of the outside surface much more than it did with old-fashioned cookware.

Measures and weights are perhaps the trickiest problem in using old cookbooks. In most of the old books, a cupful does not necessarily mean an 8-ounce cup. It could be anything from 6 to 12 ounces. Only trial and error, or long-time experience, solves this problem. Nevertheless, it is advisable to assume that a cup is 8 ounces, a wine glass 6 ounces, a shot or jigger 1 ounce—and the results will tell you how close you were.

Nor was there any standard of measure with regard to spoons. Keep in mind that soup spoons were considerably larger. A coffee spoon, sometimes mentioned in old cookbooks, is larger than a teaspoon.

Many of the older cookbooks give monetary measures—a penny's worth of yeast, a two-cent bun, or a five-cent jar. Of course these are confusing until you realize that a penny's worth of yeast was always a unit of yeast, just like today's envelope of dry yeast or cake of fresh yeast. It is easy to substitute. The bun or roll usually refers to a hard roll approximately three inches in diameter. A jar of whatever is pretty much the same as today's sizes of jars. A five-cent jar of orange jam or apricot marmalade means approximately 12 ounces.

Oven temperatures, if mentioned at all, are generalized. Low, lukewarm, or warm are ordinarily 250 to 300 degrees. Medium is from 300 to 400 degrees, but usually means 350 degrees. High starts at about 375 degrees, and can be as high as 500 degrees. Only experience can determine exactly the correct temperature in each case.

After all these considerations, if the recipe does not turn out as desired, it does not necessarily mean that the recipe is wrong. It may indicate that something that was thought to be delicious and fashionable when the book was written just does not suit present-day tastes. Some puddings, omelets, and creams, for example, are now considered too sweet, too heavy, or too rich. Gravies and sauces may seem too fat, too thick, or overspiced.

With spices in general, it is advisable to cut down on quantity; it is easy to add more if needed. Today's spices are fresher, better handled, and therefore, are more pungent and potent.

Edible plants found in Mexico. Bookplate from Dr. John Francis Gemelli Careri's travel book. Original etchings by the author, 1698.

TO FRICASSEE A SMALL CHICKEN, SOUTHERN MODE

The Improved Housewife; or Book of Receipts

By A Married Lady

A fricassee is a dish of meat that has been cut into small pieces, stewed or fried, and then cooked a while longer in a sauce prepared from its own gravy. Recipes for this type of dish appear in the very old cookbooks, even in some that were handwritten before the first cookbook was ever printed. Fricasseed chicken is certainly not an American dish, but the method used in this recipe makes it American and Southern. This dish is unusual because the chicken is cooked in wine without any other liquid, and because the sauce is made separately and then added to the chicken.

INGREDIENTS:

4 small spring chickens, 1 to 1½ pounds each

1½ tablespoons salt

½ teaspoon black pepper

¼ teaspoon mace

enough water to cover

1 cup of the cooking liquid

6 tablespoons butter (¾ stick)

2 tablespoons flour

1½ cups milk

8 tablespoons white wine

METHOD:

1. Cut up the chickens as follows: Split through the back from the tail to the neck. Lay open, skin side down. Remove the keel bone from the breast; then split the chicken into two halves. Cut off the two breasts, with the wings, then remove two joints of the wing, leaving one on the breast. Cut the drumsticks off the thighs.

2. Wash the necks, gizzard, livers, and chicken pieces, and put all into a large soup pot.
3. Add spices and water to cover; bring to a boil; reduce heat and simmer gently until tender when pierced with a fork.
4. Remove chicken from liquid.
5. Measure out one cup of the liquid, and pour it into a saucepan.
6. Blend the flour into the melted butter.
7. Bring the juices in the saucepan to a boil, then remove the pan from the heat and slowly add the butter-flour mixture in small quantities, so that it does not become lumpy. When all is added, replace over the heat and bring to a gentle boil, stirring constantly.
8. Stir in the milk and simmer just under the boiling point for 10 minutes.
9. Place all the chicken parts into a large skillet or flat pan.
10. Pour the white wine over the chicken, then slowly add the sauce, shaking the pan while adding it.
11. Stir with a wooden cooking spoon, turning the chicken pieces. Heat through but do not bring to a boil. Serve hot.

Serves 8.

Picnicking in Virginia, 1888.

TO THE FEW WHO ARE NOT OUR CUSTOMERS

Continuing to use the same flour you now have prevents obtaining all that is possible in baking

And it will be so until you make a change

Until you buy GOLD MEDAL FLOUR, we cannot help you

GOLD MEDAL FLOUR helped our customers make twenty-seven hundred million loaves last year — every loaf beautiful, creamy white with a golden bloom on the crust

Make a change and use Gold Medal Flour — because it will bring results and results are what you want and we want

WASHBURN-CROSBY CO'S
GOLD MEDAL FLOUR

Gold Medal flour advertisement, ca. 1880.

WONDERS OR CRULLERS

Directions for Cookery in its Various Branches

By Miss Leslie

Foods that could be prepared quickly were very suitable for the early American homemaker. There were no appliances and no household help, so the homemaker had to do as much as possible in as short a time as she could. This pastry is an adaptation of a much more elaborate European dough that required hours of preparation and was cut with fancy cutters into different shapes. In this recipe the simplified batter and the fast crinkle-cutter made it very suitable for an American way of life.

INGREDIENTS:

4 cups flour

¾ cup granulated sugar

½ teaspoon ground cinnamon

½ teaspoon ground nutmeg

8 tablespoons butter (1 stick)

3 eggs, slightly beaten

1 tablespoon rum (or rose water, if available)

about ½ cup sifted flour, for dusting

2 cups oil combined with 4 cups lard or other shortening, for frying

powdered sugar

METHOD:

1. Sift the flour, together with the granulated sugar, cinnamon, and nutmeg, into a bowl.
2. With two forks, cut the butter into the mixture, until it is evenly distributed and no butter particle is bigger than a coffee bean.

3. Add the slightly beaten eggs and the rum or rose water, and toss the mixture together.

4. Wash your hands in ice water and wipe dry. With *cold* hands, quickly form the mixture into a ball. No loose particles should remain in the bowl. Do not overmix.

5. Divide the ball in half; wrap each half in plastic, and chill in the refrigerator for 15 to 20 minutes.

6. Flour a pastry board and roll out one portion of the dough until it is ¼-inch thick, then cut the dough with a crinkled ravioli cutter into strips 4 inches long and ½-inch wide.

7. Repeat with the remaining portion of dough.

8. Fry the strips of dough in the preheated *hot* mixture of oil and shortening until golden brown.

9. Remove from the shortening; drain on paper towels, then sprinkle with powdered sugar and serve hot or cold.

Makes 3 dozen crullers.

Dining car of the Union Pacific Railway, 1870. Railroad dining cars were popular social gathering places for the rich.

STEWED FROG LEGS

Hand-Book of Practical Cookery for Ladies and Professional Cooks

By Pierre Blot

In Europe, frog legs were eaten as a delicacy, but in the southern and middle United States, they were a welcome staple in early times. With little effort or expense children could catch the "main ingredient" in abundance. These tasty, nutritious, and inexpensive morsels required little preparation and a very short cooking time.

INGREDIENTS:

4 tablespoons butter (one-half stick)

16 pairs large, or 24 pairs medium-sized fresh or frozen frog hind legs, skinned and blanched

1 teaspoon flour

¼ teaspoon dry thyme

pinch of white pepper and salt to taste

2 sprigs parsley

1 bay leaf

2 whole cloves, slightly bruised

1 clove garlic, mashed to a pulp with ½ teaspoon salt

1 cup dry white wine, such as Rhine wine, a dry French type like Chablis, or a California dry white wine

2 egg yolks

parsley sprigs, watercress, and lemon wedges for garnish, optional

METHOD:

1. Melt the butter in a large frying pan with a tight fitting lid.
2. Place the frog legs in the frying pan, next to each other, not on top of each other, and cover. Cook over medium heat, shaking the

pan once in awhile, for approximately 2 to 3 minutes. If the frog legs were frozen, simmer over low heat in the butter for 10 to 12 minutes.

3. Mix together the flour, thyme, salt, and white pepper; sprinkle the mixture evenly over the frog legs. Stir.

4. Add the parsley, bay leaf, cloves, and garlic paste; immediately pour in the white wine.

5. Reduce the heat to low as soon as the wine starts to boil. Cover and cook gently until a toothpick inserted into a frog leg comes out easily, and not too much juice oozes out when the toothpick is removed. This will take approximately 6 to 10 minutes, depending on the size of the frog legs and the quality of the pan.

6. Gently remove the frog legs to a serving platter.

7. Stir the sauce with a wooden spoon, then strain through a fine sieve. Discard the solids.

8. Place the two egg yolks into a warm bowl. Spoonful by spoonful, mix the hot sauce into the egg yolks. Be careful not to add too much of the hot sauce to the egg yolks at once; otherwise, the egg yolks will cook and the sauce will become lumpy.

9. Spoon the sauce over the frog legs, decorate the platter with parsley sprigs or watercress, and lemon wedges. Serve this dish immediately.

Serves 8.

"A Trouville," cartoon from French magazine, 19th century.

SWEET POTATO PUDDING

Home Cookery; A Collection of Tested Receipts

By Mrs. Chadwick

The sweet potato is a member of one plant family that is native to the southern part of North America and the northern part of South America. In the time of Columbus, it was already known in the Caribbean, and it immediately found favor with the Spanish explorers. They carried it very early to Europe, where for centuries it nonetheless remained a rarity. The first people to settle in the United States began to use it immediately, and the sweet potato became an integral part not only of cooking in the South, but throughout the eastern seaboard. It was carried westward with the spread of agriculture.

INGREDIENTS:

5 eggs

8 tablespoons butter (1 stick)

½ cup sugar

1 can, 1-pound size, sweet potatoes or whole yams

1 lemon

whipped cream or a tart fruit sauce, optional

METHOD:

1. Preheat the oven to 350 degrees.
2. Beat the eggs, butter, and sugar together, using the medium speed of an electric beater.
3. Add the cut-up sweet potatoes or yams slowly, continuing to mix on medium speed. Mix until all are combined, and the mixture is smooth.
4. Grate the lemon peeling so that no white part comes off with the outside skin.

aturday half-holiday, 1871.

5.   Add the grated zest and the juice from the lemon to the sweet potato mixture.

6.   Butter a 2-quart form. Pour the mixture into the form. Cover with a lid or aluminum foil, and place the form in a larger pan filled with water to one inch of the top of the form. Bake for 35-40 minutes.

7.   Remove from the oven and waterbath, and let stand for 5 to 10 minutes.

8.   Remove cover; place a serving dish upside down on top of the container, and turn dish and container over together, so the pudding is inverted onto the serving dish.

9.   Serve immediately with whipped cream or a tart fruit sauce.

Serves 8.

Hog industry: cutting and packing, illustration from periodical, 1860.

SAUSAGES

The New Family Book; or Ladies' Indispensable Companion

By E. Hutchinson

The idea of mincing meat and stuffing it into natural animal casings, then preserving it through smoking, curing, or other methods is as old as the first attempts of people to domesticate cattle, sheep, and pigs. But this variety of sausage, heavily flavored by the pungency of dry sage, is very American. So is the fact that it is prepared without a casing. This recipe is not primarily about a method of preserving, as in the Old World; rather, it is a method of quickly preparing cuts of meat which would ordinarily need much longer cooking. Speed and convenience make this recipe very American.

INGREDIENTS:

1 pound lean pork shoulder

1 pound lean boneless pork loin

1 tablespoon salt

½ teaspoon ground black pepper

¼ teaspoon ground white pepper

1 teaspoon rubbed (powdered) sage

¼ teaspoon powdered basil

1 pinch garlic salt

1 cup lukewarm water

¼ cup sifted flour

METHOD:

1. Grind the pork meats twice, using the medium blade of a meat grinder.
2. Dissolve all the spices and herbs in the water.
3. Add the water-spice mixture to the ground pork, and work with your hands to knead together until completely mixed.

4.   Sprinkle half of the flour through a sieve over the pork mixture. Work it into the mixture; then repeat with the second half of the flour.

5.   Let the mixture stand at room temperature for 30 minutes, then refrigerate.

6.   After at least 1 hour of chilling, remove and place the mixture on a cutting board. Shape into a 1-inch high square.

7.   Using a wet knife, divide the mixture into 16 equal parts.

8.   Roll each portion between wet palms into sausages approximately 2½ inches long. Refrigerate.

9.   To serve, place as many sausages as needed in a frying pan that has been rinsed in cold water. Place over medium heat; cover, and cook for 5 to 6 minutes. Remove cover; increase heat, and fry until browned, or for an additional 6 to 8 minutes.

10. Drain on absorbent paper towels and serve immediately.

Makes 16 sausages.

"Sunday in New Orleans — The French Market," Harper's Weekly, *1866.*

Ladies' and children's aprons, 1870s.

PEACH SAUCE

Mrs. Porter's New Southern Cookery Book

By Mrs. Porter

Peaches were not native to the Western Hemisphere but were brought by the Spaniards to Louisiana and Florida very early. From there they spread quickly. When Captain Smith arrived in the New World, he reported finding peach trees. Peaches became an important agricultural crop early on, especially in Georgia and also in the other southern states. Because the peach has a short ripening time, it was necessary to dry them in the sun to preserve them. This very simple recipe, which uses unrefined cane sugar (brown sugar) as the only other ingredient besides water, made this sauce traditionally American.

INGREDIENTS:

1-pound package dried peaches

2 cups hot water

1 cup brown sugar

METHOD:

1. Place the peaches in a glass or plastic container, and add enough lukewarm water to cover. Let stand for 2 hours.
2. Pour off the water; rinse the peaches, and add fresh lukewarm water to cover again. Let stand overnight.
3. Next day, discard the water. Chop the peaches into small dice.
4. Place 1 cup of hot water in a heavy sauce pan. Add the peaches; bring to a simmering, slow boil; cover and cook over low heat, stirring occasionally, for 1 hour. Add more water only if necessary.
5. Dissolve the brown sugar in the remaining cup of hot water, then add the mixture to the peaches. Bring to a boil again, stirring constantly, then remove and cool.
6. Chill and serve with roast meats, poultry, and game.

Makes 1 quart.

"Pictures of the South—Barbeque at Atlanta, Georgia," illustration from periodical, ca. *1880.*

MISSISSIPPI CORN BREAD

Presbyterian Cook Book

Compiled by the Ladies of the First Presbyterian Church,

Dayton, Ohio

Corn was domesticated by American Indians in pre-Columbian times from a native American plant. It quickly became the staple of most agricultural Indian tribes. The Indians also used corn to barter with the early settlers. Corn bread was an early American staple, and in certain places in the South it is still preferred to any other type of starch food or bread.

INGREDIENTS:

8 tablespoons butter (1 stick)

1 pound cooked rice (6 ounces rice, boiled in 3 cups water, for 30 minutes)

1 pound cornmeal

1 teaspoon salt

2 cups buttermilk, mixed with 1 teaspoon baking soda

METHOD:

1. Preheat oven to 400 degrees. Butter a 10-inch round (or equivalent size) pan.
2. Melt butter, and then combine with rice, cornmeal, salt, and buttermilk mixture. Beat with a wooden spoon until well blended.
3. Pour the batter into a buttered pan and bake in preheated oven for 20 minutes; then reduce heat to 375 degrees and bake for 20 more minutes. Serve hot.

Serves 6 — 8.

Outdoor barbeque in San Antonio, Texas, during a folk festival, 1882.

MEXICAN EGGS

Capitol City Cook Book

By The Grace Church Woman's Guild

Bell peppers and tomatoes both were domesticated by pre-Columbian Indians. European settlers learned about their usage from the Indians, especially in Texas, New Mexico, Arizona, and areas south. That is why dishes prepared with tomatoes and bell peppers are considered Mexican in many parts of the country. The French and Spanish made these two vegetables an integral part of their American cuisine. And that cuisine, characteristically American, is known today as Creole. Where dishes prepared with tomatoes and peppers are not called Mexican, as in the *Capitol City Cook Book,* they are called Creole.

INGREDIENTS:

2 tablespoons butter or bacon drippings

2 tablespoons finely chopped bell pepper

2 tablespoons finely chopped onion

1 can 1-pound size stewed tomatoes, drained
(liquid can be saved for later use)

½ teaspoon salt

16 eggs, slightly beaten, with ½ cup milk or light cream

Tabasco sauce, optional

METHOD:

1. Heat the butter or bacon drippings in a skillet.
2. Add the chopped pepper and onion, stir, and cook for 2 to 3 minutes.

3. Add the drained tomatoes and salt. Stir, cutting up the tomatoes with the spoon. Cook slowly for 6 to 8 minutes, until bubbling and hot.

4. Quickly add the egg-milk mixture all at once, and keep stirring and cooking just until the eggs set. Do not let them become dry.

5. Add a few drops of Tabasco sauce if you like the eggs hot. Serve with chorizos, a Mexican-type sausage, or with other spicy meats.

Serves 8.

New York beer garden in Central Park, 1876.

DRESDEN DRESSING

Six Little Cooks; or Aunt Jane's Cooking Class

By Elizabeth Stansbury Kirkland

One would wonder—and justifiably—about finding among American recipes something named after the famous German city of painting, sculpture, and china manufacture. But Dresden Dressing is American. Most likely, the person who named it came from Dresden, or named it to honor that city. It is a dressing only in the old American sense of the word, because it is not what we now call a "dressing," meaning salad dressing. It is actually a cold sauce or condiment, meant to accompany cold beef, mutton, veal, or cold cuts.

INGREDIENTS:

3 hard-boiled eggs
⅓ cup finely grated or finely minced onion
2 tablespoons chopped green parsley
1 scant teaspoon salt
1 scant teaspoon sugar
1 pinch dry mustard
¼ cup corn oil
¼ cup white vinegar

METHOD:

1.   Separate the yolks from the egg whites.
2.   If a greyish layer covers the egg yolks, submerge them in lukewarm water and gently rub the surface with your thumb until the greyish substance loosens, then pat dry on a kitchen towel or absorbent paper.
3.   Rub the yolks through a fine sieve into a mixing bowl.
4.   Combine the yolks with the onion, parsley, salt, sugar, and dry mustard.

5. Slowly add the oil, beating at high speed with an electric mixer, first adding drop by drop, and then pouring in a slow thin stream.

6. Keep beating until the mixture thickens, then reduce the speed to low and slowly add the vinegar.

7. Correct seasoning by adding a little more sugar, salt, or dry mustard, depending on your taste.

8. Transfer the dressing to a small glass container, and chill. Serve as an accompaniment to cold beef, mutton, veal, or cold cuts.

Note: Meat can be cut into thin julienne strips or small cubes and gently folded into the dressing. Or more simply, slice the meat and offer the dressing separately. If you wish, add the coarsely chopped egg whites, or use the egg whites for decoration.

Makes 1 cup.

The dining room of the Fifth Avenue H
on Madison Square, Harper's Weekly, *18*

An American hotel dining room as seen through the eyes of an Englishman, sketched by Randolph Caldecott, from a British magazine, ca. *1870.*

BOILED FOWL

The Kansas Home Cook Book

Compiled by C. H. Cushing and Mrs. B. Gray

This intriguing recipe may be of English origin, but it is never found in English books cooked this way. It tastes much better than it sounds.

INGREDIENTS:

1 stewing hen or a young fowl, 4-5 pounds

salt and white pepper, according to taste

¼ teaspoon garlic salt, optional

4 tablespoons butter (one-half stick)

2 dozen shucked oysters

1 tablespoon flour

½ cup light cream or milk

1 tablespoon chopped fresh green parsley

METHOD:

1. Quickly wash the fowl, inside and outside; rinse and pat dry.
2. Rub it with a little salt, white pepper, and, if you wish, a light sprinkling of garlic salt.
3. Put half the butter into a soup pot (if possible, a pot that is taller than it is wide) that has a tight-fitting lid.
4. Place the fowl in the pot, then pour the oysters, including their liquid, into the cavity of the fowl.
5. Cover the pot and place it into a much larger pot. Fill the larger pot with boiling water that comes to within 1 inch of the top.
6. Place over medium heat, cover the larger pot, and keep gently boiling for 1 hour, 30 minutes. Check for doneness—if a bamboo skewer or a strong round toothpick inserted into the thickest part of the thigh comes out hot and a perfectly clear juice oozes, the fowl is done. There should be no trace of pinkness to the juice.

7. Stir the flour into the cream or milk, and let it stand.

8. When the chicken is done, gently remove the smaller pot from the boiling water.

9. Using two towels, open the lid a little bit and pour the liquid off into another saucepan.

10. Remove the lid completely, and gently slide the whole fowl onto a large, shallow serving dish. Let stand for a few minutes, then add the liquid that oozes onto the serving dish to the liquid in the saucepan.

11. Add the remaining butter to the juices.

12. With a wire whip, stir the cream-flour (or milk-flour) mixture into the juices in the saucepan.

13. Place the mixture over medium heat and bring to a boil, stirring constantly with the whip. As soon as it begins to boil, remove from the heat and let steep for 10 minutes.

14. Spoon the sauce over the fowl; sprinkle with freshly chopped parsley, and serve with fluffy rice or boiled potatoes, Mississippi Corn Bread (page 75), Baked Stuffed Potatoes (page 111), or Tomato Marmalade (page 103).

Serves 8.

HASHED LITTLE NECK CLAMS ON TOAST

One Hundred Recipes for the Chafing Dish

By H. M. Kinsley

This recipe was created shortly after canning was perfected, most likely by an American home economist working for a canning company.

INGREDIENTS:

4 tablespoons butter (½ stick)

2 cans, 8-ounce size, minced clams

1 teaspoon freshly chopped green parsley

1 teaspoon freshly chopped chives or ¼ teaspoon dried chives

salt and freshly ground black pepper, according to taste

*⅓ cup dry white bread crumbs, made from
Italian or French bread*

¼ cup sherry

8 slices toast, buttered or plain

METHOD:

1. Melt the butter in a frying pan or chafing dish.
2. When the butter is hot, add the minced clams, including their juice, herbs, salt, and pepper.
3. Cover and bring to a boil, then add bread crumbs and sherry. Stir until the mixture thickens.
4. Correct seasoning, if necessary, by adding more salt or pepper. Divide over the slices of toast, and serve hot.

Serves 8.

Vermont farmer collecting maple sap on a horse-drawn sled, original etching from German publication, 1873.

SWEET POTATO WAFFLES

High Living

By L. L. McLaren

What an ironic twist to use the waffle iron, which was invented in Europe, with a real American main ingredient such as the sweet potato! The waffles come out of the iron nicely browned and crisp. Lovers of sweet potatoes, as well as gourmets, are in for a treat.

INGREDIENTS:

2 cups mashed, boiled sweet potatoes

2 eggs, separated

½ cup granulated sugar

1 cup melted, warm butter

2 cups milk

4 to 6 tablespoons flour

shortening to brush waffle iron

METHOD:

1. Mash sweet potatoes through a sieve.
2. Beat the two egg yolks, then stir them into the sweet potatoes.
3. Beat the whites with a wire whip until they form soft peaks, then fold them into the potato mixture.
4. Add the sugar; beat again, then slowly pour in the melted butter, alternating with the milk and continuing to beat.
5. Fold as much flour as needed into the batter to make it as thick as a pancake batter.
6. Bake waffles on high heat in the buttered iron.

Makes 8 waffles.

Scene with American Indians, from 17th-century travel book. Note the hanging fish, finger-sized bananas, and the squash used as a drinking cup.

SWEET POTATO BUNS

Cooking in Old Creole Days

By Celestine Eustis

When the first Spaniards arrived, sweet potatoes were already one of the great agricultural staples of the American Indians. These buns, made from sweet potatoes, are remarkably tasty. Their spongy texture and their vivid orange color adds an interesting note to any assorted bread basket.

INGREDIENTS:

3 tablespoons lukewarm water

1 package dry yeast

pinch of sugar

1 can yams, 1-pound, 4-ounce size, rinsed and patted dry

1 cup sifted flour

4 tablespoons butter, at room temperature

additional flour for dusting

METHOD:

1. Preheat oven to 400 degrees.
2. Dissolve yeast in water; add sugar, then set aside to rise.
3. Mash the yams in a bowl, then add the yeast mixture and half the flour.
4. Work the mixture together with your hands, then add the second half of the flour and mix in.
5. Place the mixture in a bowl dusted with flour; cover, and set aside in a warm place until it has risen.
6. Remove the dough to a lightly floured board, and knead in the butter.

7.   Divide the dough into 12 equal portions (or more if smaller buns are desired); shape each into a round, and place on a buttered sheet pan.

8.   Cover with a towel and let rise again.

9.   Bake in the preheated oven for 20 to 25 minutes, or until done. Serve with butter.

Makes 12 buns.

The new West Washington food market, New York City, Harper's Weekly, *1888.*

HAM AND SWEET POTATO SALAD

Priscilla Cook Book

Compiled by the Christian Church Priscilla Aid

The American homemaker, for whom time is money, has created great dishes that require no cooking. Just as often, she leaves the cooking to the manufacturer. As soon as she buys the ingredients, all she needs is a knife for cubing and a spoon for mixing. In this case, a very satisfying and nourishing dish is created without spending very much time on it.

INGREDIENTS:

2 cups diced, cooked ham, cut into ½-inch cubes
2 cups diced, cooked sweet potato, cut into ½-inch cubes
1 cup diced celery, cut in ¼-inch dice
1 cup apple, cut in ¼-inch dice
1 cup fresh orange sections
¼ cup chopped pecans (optional)
1 cup mayonnaise

METHOD:

1. Gently combine all the ingredients, adding the sweet potatoes last to avoid smashing them.
2. Chill and serve in large lettuce leaves.
3. If you wish, serve with additional mayonnaise.

Serves 8.

"New York City—The Camp of Company H., Fifth U.S. Artillery, On Guard at the Tomb of General Grant, Riverside Park—Preparing Supper," Frank Leslie's Illustrated Newspaper, *1885.*

POTATO DRESSING

Florida Salads

By Francis Barber Harris

Potato salad may not go along with the current American fad for dieting, but it is a very old American dish. This recipe is a slightly different way to include potatoes in a meal.

INGREDIENTS:

1 boiled, medium-sized potato, still warm

2 yolks of hard-boiled eggs

1 teaspoon butter

½ teaspoon prepared mustard

salt, according to taste

½ cup white vinegar

1 cup corn oil or olive oil

2 teaspoons sugar

1 tablespoon lemon juice

few drops onion juice

Tabasco sauce, according to taste

METHOD:

1. Mash the potato and egg yolks through an enamel colander.
2. While this mixture is still warm, add the butter, mustard, and salt. Chill.
3. Prepare a vinaigrette dressing by combining the vinegar, oil, sugar, lemon juice, onion juice, and Tabasco sauce.
4. Combine the two mixtures to form a smooth dressing. Serve.

Makes 3 cups.

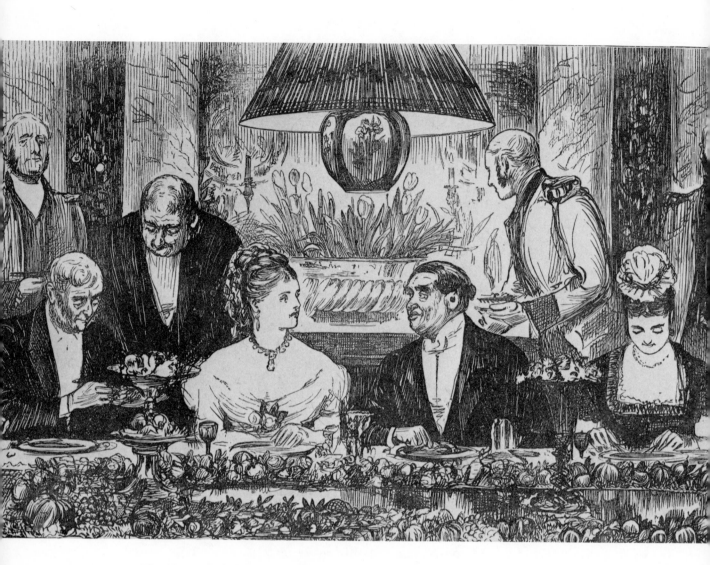

The business of pleasure, undated.

GRAPEFRUIT AND LOBSTER SALAD

Electric Refrigerator Recipes & Menus

By Miss Alice Bradley

Among the edible blessings of the oceans, perhaps nothing is as American as Maine lobster. It lives only on the northeast and east coast of the North American continent. Lobster may be prepared in many different ways. Combined with grapefruit is one of the most enjoyable.

INGREDIENTS:

4 large grapefruits

2 lobsters, 1½-2 pounds each, or 4 lobster tails, 7-8 ounces each

½ cup finely minced celery, if possible the hearts

2 tablespoons finely chopped pecans

*1 cup mayonnaise-type salad dressing, or
the same amount of homemade mayonnaise*

1 bunch watercress

METHOD:

1.   Cut each grapefruit into two half-crowns, or simply cut each in half crosswise.
2.   With a grapefruit knife, carefully remove all the segments and place them in a bowl.
3.   With kitchen scissors, cut out every second membrane attached to the grapefruit peeling.
4.   Replace every second piece of grapefruit section, and fill the remaining empty spaces with boiled and sliced cold lobster meat.
5.   Mix the celery, pecans, and mayonnaise together. Fill the middle of each grapefruit half with this mixture.
6.   Sprinkle the edges with finely chopped watercress.

7.   Chill and serve on individual plates, garnished if you wish with chicory lettuce, additional watercress, or any other green of your choice.

Note: If you wish, use cooked shrimp instead of the lobster. In this case, you would need approximately 6 medium-sized shrimps per person.

Serves 8.

Oyster stands in the Fulton Market, a popular stop for shopping ladies. Harper's Weekly, *1870.*

OYSTER SHORTCAKE

A Collection of Choice Recipes

Contributed by the Ladies of Des Moines

Shortcake is the most American of all baked doughs, even more so than pie pastry. Combined with fresh oysters it makes a delightful, typically American dish.

INGREDIENTS FOR CRUST:

2 cups flour

2 teaspoons baking powder

½ teaspoon salt

¾ cup milk, at room temperature

2 tablespoons melted butter

INGREDIENTS FOR FILLING:

1 pint shucked oysters, or equivalent in canned oysters

2 tablespoons water

3 tablespoons butter

3 tablespoons flour

1 ½ cups milk

salt and freshly ground black pepper, according to taste

METHOD:

1. Preheat oven to 350 degrees.
2. For the crust, sift together the flour, baking powder, and salt.
3. Very quickly work in 2 teaspoons of the butter and the milk. Do not overwork.
4. Butter an 8 inch by 1½-inch round cake pan.
5. Divide the dough in two, and gently pat half into the bottom of the pan.

6. Brush the dough in the pan with half of the remaining butter, then pat the second half of the dough on top.

7. Brush the top with the remaining butter and bake for approximately 30 to 35 minutes.

8. Remove from oven and cool. Invert pan to remove shortcake, then immediately turn over so the top is up again. Let stand in a warm place.

9. If fresh oysters are used in the filling, scald them in a small saucepan with their own juice until the edges curl, adding a few tablespoons of water if necessary. Remove immediately from the heat and keep warm.

10. Melt the butter in a saucepan.

11. Mix the flour into the milk. When the butter starts to sizzle, slowly pour the flour-milk mixture into the hot butter, stirring constantly with a wire whip.

12. Bring the mixture to a boil for a few seconds, then reduce the heat to low. Add salt and freshly ground black pepper, and fold in the scalded or canned oysters. Heat through.

13. Gently separate the two halves of the shortcake with a fork, breaking apart where the butter was brushed in the middle.

14. Place the bottom part on a large round serving platter or in a 9-inch ovenproof pie plate.

15. Divide the bottom into eight pieces, as you would cut a pie, gently pulling it apart with two forks.

16. Ladle the hot oyster sauce over the shortcake.

17. Cut the top half like the bottom, and arrange the pieces so that each top and bottom piece fits together.

18. Decorate with a few sprigs of parsley, if desired, and place a thick slice of lemon on each if you wish. Serve hot with additional freshly ground pepper.

Serves 8.

BEECH-NUT
PEANUT BUTTER

NEVER refuse a child Beech-Nut Peanut Butter. The child's nature longs for it, and the child naturally demands it.

Peanut Butter flavor has an affinity for air, but Beech-Nut Airless Sealing claps a lid on the glass jar quick and tight, and holds the flavor till you spring the lid off.

You'll like it like the "kids" do, on bread or crackers, etc. Nourishing, too. Nothing in it but peanuts and salt, ground to a creamy golden brown butter. Try a 15c jar from your grocer *today*. But *insist* on Beech-Nut brand.

For Children After School, Fine.

Made by the makers of famous Beech-Nut Bacon. Visit the clean, sunny Beech-Nut plant in the picturesque Mohawk Valley. Beech-Nut Packing Company, Canajoharie, N. Y.

Shortly after a St. Louis dentist invented peanut butter, this great American food was widely advertised by manufacturers.

PEANUT BRITTLE DESSERT

Dorcas Cook Book

Published by the Dorcas Society of St. John Lutheran Church

The peanut or earth nut is a plant native to the Western Hemisphere. It is conceded throughout the world that it was first cultivated in the United States. Today, when many African countries consider the peanut of utmost importance, and virtually all other countries value it as one of the most important sources of vegetable protein and oils, it is hard to believe that it was introduced to the Old World less than three hundred years ago. This recipe is a delightful and ingenious concoction, using another very American ingredient, the marshmallow, and something very naturally fresh—whipped cream.

INGREDIENTS:

20 marshmallows

1 cup heavy cream

¾ cup peanut brittle, ground or finely chopped

METHOD:

1. Chill eight parfait glasses.
2. Using scissors, cut the marshmallows in quarters.
3. Whip the cream until it is stiff, but do not overbeat it.
4. Gently fold the marshmallows and half of the peanut brittle into the whipped cream.
5. Chill the mixture in the mixing bowl for 1 to 1½ hours.
6. Spoon the mixture into the chilled glasses, and chill for an additional hour or longer.
7. To serve, decorate the top of each with a sprinkling of the additional chopped peanut brittle.

Serves 8.

The Centennial Banquet in Horticultural Hall, Philadelphia, Harper's Weekly, *1876.*

TOMATO MARMALADE

Patriotic Food Show Official Recipe Book

By the Women's Central Committee on Food Conservation

The legendary love apple, or tomato, grew in abundance throughout the Western Hemisphere from earliest times. To preserve it in the form of marmalade, jam, or jelly was a natural idea for the American homemaker.

INGREDIENTS:

12 medium-sized tomatoes, approximately 2 ½ inches in diameter and 1 ¾ to 2 inches high, ripened but still firm

2 small, thin-skinned lemons

2 cups sugar

1 quart boiling water

METHOD:

1. Preheat oven to 350 degrees.
2. Bring the water to a boil over high heat in a 2-quart pan.
3. Next to the stove have a pan containing 2 to 3 quarts of cold water and a dozen ice cubes.
4. Put 3 tomatoes into the boiling water, one by one, slowly submerging them with a slotted spoon. Cover for 3 to 4 seconds, then lift out and immediately place in the ice water.
5. Repeat until all the tomatoes have been scalded and cooled.
6. Peel each tomato with a sharp, thin paring knife. Discard peel and core.
7. Cut the tomatoes in half crosswise, and gently remove as many seeds as possible.
8. Turn the tomato halves upside down on absorbent paper to drain.
9. Cut the two lemons into quarters, and remove the seeds and the white pulp that runs through the middle of the lemon.

10. Slice the quartered lemon pieces crosswise, very thin, with a sharp knife. It is best if you slice them into a shallow plastic dish so all the juice is saved.

11. If the skin of the lemon has too much white pulp, peel off the yellow outside, discarding the white part. Then, slice the yellow skin into thin strips; slice the lemon quarters into thin slices.

12. In an enameled pot or an ovenproof dish, place a layer of sliced tomatoes, followed by some lemon slices. Continue to so layer until all the tomatoes and lemon slices are used.

13. Distribute the two cups of sugar evenly over the top.

14. Cover the dish and put it in the oven for 4 hours, without disturbing it.

15. After 4 hours, increase the temperature to 400 degrees; remove the lid; stir, and bake for an additional 15 to 30 minutes, or until the mixture thickens. The time will vary, depending on the percentage of liquid in the tomatoes.

16. Pack in hot sterilized jars, as you would pack any other home-made marmalade. Alternately, spread into a thin layer in a glass or plastic dish; cool quickly, and then refrigerate in a closed plastic jar. The marmalade will keep refrigerated for one month.

Makes 1 quart.

ROUND STEAK SAUSAGE FORCEMEAT

Y.M.C.A. Cook Book

Compiled by the Young Men's Christian Association

Steaks stuffed with American bulk pork sausage are unknown in any other part of the world. This is a genuinely American idea and a great gastronomical victory. The result is tantalizing and very different.

INGREDIENTS:

2 round steaks, 1 pound each, well trimmed and as lean
as possible (save trimmings)
salt and freshly ground black pepper to taste
1 pound bulk pork sausage
1 cup soft, white bread crumbs, tightly packed
2 tablespoons flour
2 to 3 tablespoons bacon drippings, plus all fat trimmings from the steaks
1 to 2 cups soup stock, canned consommé, or water
8 to 10 medium-sized potatoes, peeled and halved

METHOD:

1. Pound each steak thin with a mallet, being careful not to make holes in the meat.
2. Sprinkle each steak with a little salt and grind fresh black pepper over each.
3. Mix the bulk sausage with the breadcrumbs.
4. Add 1 to 2 tablespoons liquid, as necessary, to make an even, moist filling.
5. Taste the sausage mixture and add more seasoning if you wish, such as finely minced onion, garlic salt or powder, sage, sweet basil, etc.
6. Divide the sausage mixture in half, and cover each steak with a portion of it, patting it out with the palm of your hand so it doesn't get too close to the edges of the steak.

7.   Roll up each steak and secure the ends with small metal skewers, strong round toothpicks, or bamboo skewers.

8.   Dredge both steaks with flour.

9.   Heat the bacon drippings and the fat trimmings in a large frying pan.

10.   Add steaks and sear, rolling them over until all areas are nicely browned and crusty.

11.   Place the steaks in a roasting pan with a cover, or in a Dutch oven, and pour in 1 to 1½ cups stock (or whatever liquid is used). The amount will depend on the size of the pan.

12.   Roast, covered, on top of the stove, or roast in a preheated 400-degree oven. If roasting in the oven, baste every 15 to 20 minutes.

13.   After 45 minutes, place the potatoes around the roast and baste the potatoes with the liquid.

14.   If all the liquid evaporates, add more.

15.   Roast for an additional 15 to 25 minutes, or until the potatoes are fork tender and the beef is done. The timing will depend very much on the quality of the meat, therefore it is advisable to keep checking for tenderness.

16.   When ready, remove the meat to a carving board and let it cool somewhat, then remove skewers and slice each roll with a sharp knife into eight even slices. Each portion will be 2 slices of the round steak rouladen and 2 potato halves.

17.   Arrange the potatoes around the meat. Serve with a salad or green vegetable.

Serves 8.

Armour Calendar, 1893.

A New England cider mill with horsedrawn press, undated.

APPLE CATSUP

Library Ann's Cook Book

Compiled by the Minneapolis Public Library Staff Association

Just as catsup is very American, so is the idea of making it from apples instead of tomatoes. This recipe looks strange, but if you prepare it, you will be surprised at what a great relish it is with roast pork, baked ham, and many other main course dishes.

INGREDIENTS:

12 large, firm, tart apples

1 cup sugar

1 teaspoon white pepper

1 teaspoon ground cloves

1 teaspoon dry mustard

2 medium-sized white onions, finely minced

2 cups white pickling vinegar

2 teaspoons cinnamon

1 tablespoon salt

½ cup prepared horseradish

METHOD:

1. Pare, core, and cut the apples into quarters.
2. Place the apples in a pot, cover with water, and cook slowly, without a lid, until apples are soft, and the water has almost completely evaporated.
3. Rub the apples through a sieve, or run through a vegetable mill.
4. Measure the amount of pulp. It should be approximately 1 quart.

5. Add all the other ingredients; heat to the boiling point; then reduce heat to low, and simmer slowly for one hour.

6. Seal in jars, or place in plastic containers which have tight fitting lids, and keep refrigerated. This catsup is especially good served with roast pork, baked ham, roast goose, or roast duck.

Makes 1 quart.

Illustration from a short story in **Harper's Weekly**, *ca.* *1900.*

BAKED STUFFED POTATOES

Choice Recipes by Moscow Women

Compiled by the Hospitality Committee of the

Presbyterian Ladies' Aid

Baked stuffed potatoes are the kind of hearty and filling invention that the early American homemaker created when the family budget was tight. It is highly recommended under any circumstances, because it is different, tasty, and easy to prepare.

INGREDIENTS:

8 large, round potatoes, 2½ to 3 inches in diameter

2 slices of bacon, cut in ¼-inch pieces

3 tablespoons finely chopped onions

3 tablespoons finely chopped celery

salt and freshly ground black pepper to taste

1 pound ground beef

1 cup milk

2 cups boiling water

1 teaspoon flour dissolved in an additional ½ cup milk

chopped parsley, optional

METHOD:

1. Preheat oven to 400 degrees.
2. Peel potatoes, and cut a slice from the ends of each so they will stand.
3. Carefully hollow out potatoes, first using a paring knife, then a melonball cutter.
4. Place the bacon in a cold frying pan, and place the pan over medium heat.
5. Fry the bacon until the pieces turn glossy and become translucent.

6. Increase heat; add onions and celery.

7. Keep stirring and cooking over high heat until the edges of the onion and celery start to brown, then reduce heat and sauté for 3 to 4 minutes.

8. Add salt and pepper, and pour the mixture over the ground beef in a mixing bowl.

9. Add the cup of milk and knead with wet hands until the mixture is completely smooth.

10. Divide the meat mixture into 8 equal portions.

11. Stuff each potato with one portion of the meat mixture.

12. Place potatoes in a greased ovenproof dish; add boiling water; and bake for 45 to 50 minutes, basting twice.

13. Remove from oven; transfer potatoes to a serving dish.

14. Pour the milk-flour mixture into the baking dish and place over low heat, stirring until thickened.

15. Pour gravy over potatoes and serve piping hot. If desired, sprinkle with freshly chopped green parsley.

Serves 8.

CHILI

The Junior League of Dallas Cook Book

Compiled by the Association of Junior Leagues of America,

Dallas Chapter

Chili is the undisputed favorite dish of the great state of Texas, but how and when the original recipe appeared is unknown. There is a secret to making this recipe: use scissors to cut the steak into small pieces, instead of chopping it on a block or grinding it through a machine. This gives the meat an entirely different texture and adds juiciness to every morsel.

INGREDIENTS:
½ pound salt pork

5-6 cups water

1 can cream of tomato soup, 10½-ounce size

1½ cups chili beans (or, if not available, use a No. 2 can kidney beans with 1 teaspoon chili powder added)

½ clove garlic

2 teaspoons cumin seeds

2 pounds round steak or similar cut

salt, according to taste

additional chili powder to taste

flour to dredge meat and onions

3-4 medium-sized onions

1-2 red bell peppers

METHOD:

1. Finely mince the salt pork.
2. Place the minced salt pork in a large soup pot with a lid, and render it over medium heat.

3. Pour off and reserve some of the fat; then add the water, tomato soup, and chili beans (which have been soaked overnight if the dried variety is used), along with the garlic and cumin seeds.

4. Simmer slowly until the beans are done.

5. With a good kitchen scissors, cut the steak into very small pieces.

6. Sprinkle the meat with some salt, chili powder, and dredge with flour.

7. Finely chop the onions; dust with flour; and set aside.

8. Heat the reserved fat in a frying pan or skillet.

9. Add the meat to the hot shortening, and sauté until done, stirring occasionally. Then add to the soup pot.

10. Fry the onions the same way and add to the soup pot.

11. Simmer the whole mixture for 10 to 15 minutes, correct seasoning if necessary, and serve.

Serves 8.

"Social Science—Cooking our Own Dinner." After the Civil War, a faddist interest developed in food and cooking; the schools also provided an excellent meeting place for eligible young men and women.

BUTTERSCOTCH CAKE PUDDING

Favorite Recipes of Colfax County Club Women

By Colfax County Club Women

The ingredients might come from anywhere in the world, but the method of this unique cake pudding is definitely American. Its successful preparation requires an electric mixer, a common tool in most every household here but a real rarity in European kitchens.

INGREDIENTS FOR THE SYRUP:

1 cup brown sugar

1 tablespoon butter

1¾ cups boiling water

INGREDIENTS FOR THE CAKE:

½ cup sugar

1 tablespoon butter, room temperature

1 cup flour

2 teaspoons baking powder

½ cup milk

1 teaspoon cinnamon, optional

½ teaspoon nutmeg, optional

½ cup raisins, optional

whipped cream, optional

METHOD:

1. Preheat the oven to 350 degrees.
2. To prepare the syrup, add the brown sugar and butter to the boiling water, stirring until sugar dissolves.
3. Bring the mixture to a boil again, reduce heat, and simmer for 5 minutes, or until the syrup coats a spoon. Cool.

Old advertisement, late 19th century.

4. To prepare the cake, combine the sugar, butter, flour, and baking powder in the bowl of an electric mixer.
5. Slowly stir in some of the milk; then start to beat on medium speed, adding the remaining milk. Beat only until smooth.
6. With a rubber spatula, fold in the spices and raisins, if desired.
7. Pour the cooled syrup into a 1½ quart casserole dish.
8. Spoon the batter into the center of the syrup, and bake in the preheated oven for 35 minutes, or until a cake tester inserted into the cake comes out dry.
9. Let cool for about 15 minutes, then invert onto a serving dish.
10. Serve warm or cold, garnished with whipped cream if desired.

Serves 6.

Black home, ca. 19th century.

WILD ONIONS AND EGGS

The Indian Cook Book

By the Indian Women's Club

According to some linguists, the name of my favorite American city, Chicago, derives from the Indian word "checagou," meaning wild onion. True or not, the fact is that wild onions are a native American plant—not to be found in any other part of the world, which, until now, have always defeated domestication. If you are lucky enough to find a place where wild onion grows, you will be able to secure, year after year, enough for the household. They freeze well.

INGREDIENTS:

2 bunches wild onions, 10 to 12 in each bunch

4 slices ranch-style bacon, thickly sliced, cut into ½-inch strips

2 tablespoons water

8 eggs

½ cup milk

salt and freshly ground black pepper, according to taste

METHOD:

1. Wash onions, remove the outer leaf, and peel the root.
2. Cut the green parts to a 2-inch lengths.
3. Coarsely chop the onions.
4. Place the chopped onions in a cold frying pan along with the pieces of bacon and fry over medium heat, stirring once in awhile, until bacon starts to turn brown and onion becomes limp.
5. Add water and a sprinkling of salt, and continue cooking for another 10 to 15 minutes.
6. Beat the eggs with the milk, salt and pepper to taste, then add to the onion mixture. Scramble fast and serve immediately.

Note: Wild onions grow throughout at least two-thirds of the United States. If you cannot find any, you may substitute one bunch of scallions, a piece of garlic the size of a small Spanish peanut, and 1 tablespoon chopped chives (fresh or frozen). Mash the garlic with salt. Chop scallions and chives together, then mix with the garlic salt. This mixture will fairly resemble the flavor of wild onions.

Serves 8.

Interior of John Howard Payne home, 1872. Payne was the author of "Home, Sweet Home." From Eastern Long Island *magazine, 1872.*

BURNT SUGAR CAKE

The Garfield Woman's Club Cook Book

By the Garfield Woman's Club

The ingenious American homemaker dreamed up this different and interesting cake. It makes a great accompaniment for afternoon coffee or a wonderful dinner dessert.

INGREDIENTS FOR BURNT SUGAR:

1 cup sugar

1 cup water

INGREDIENTS FOR THE CAKE:

2 cups sugar

1 scant cup butter

4 egg yolks, lightly beaten

5 cups flour

3 teaspoonsful baking powder

2 cups water

few drops of vanilla

¼ cup burnt sugar (or more, depending on taste)

METHOD:

1. To prepare the burnt sugar, place the sugar in a saucepan and melt it over medium heat, letting it brown.
2. As soon as sugar has melted and browned, very carefully (be sure to use a long handled ladle or pan) pour in the water. If the water is added too fast or carelessly, the sugar will spatter and can cause serious burns.
3. After water is added, stir until the crystallized sugar dissolves; then boil until the liquid is reduced to about ¾ of a cup.
4. Cool and store refrigerated, ready for use.

5.   Preheat the oven to 350 degrees. Grease and dust with flour two 8-inch cake pans.

6.   To prepare the cake, cream the butter and sugar together in the bowl of an electric mixer.

7.   Beat in the egg yolks.

8.   Sift the flour and baking powder together.

9.   Beating on low speed, alternately add the flour mixture and water, beating just until both items are incorporated and the batter is smooth.

10.   Add a few drops vanilla, then add the burnt sugar. The batter should be a rich brown color.

11.   Pour the batter into the pans; then bake in the preheated oven for 30 minutes.

12.   Cool slightly before removing from pans.

Serves 6 – 8.

TO POT CHEESE

The Improved Housewife; or Book of Receipts

By A Married Lady

Cheese making was not a New World invention, but the American homemaker, out of necessity, began to experiment with new and different methods to pot and preserve cheese. Just like the cheese manufacturer, the home cheese maker had to rework her Old World formulas, changing her accustomed methods to produce new cheeses under new circumstances.

This recipe was originally used to preserve cheese that was on the verge of molding. Of course, with today's refrigerators and freezers, it is no longer necessary to pot cheese to save it. Nevertheless, this pot cheese is a wonderful spread. Tasty and delicious, it will evoke childhood memories, or it will produce new taste sensations authentically identical with the taste our great-grandparents enjoyed.

INGREDIENTS:

1 pound soft or semi-soft cheese, such as Port Salut
1 tablespoon brandy or good bourbon

METHOD:

1.   Grate the cheese through the large holes of a four-sided kitchen grater into the mixing bowl of an electric mixer that has a paddle or dough hook. Do not use a wire whip.
2.   On slow speed, mix the cheese with the liquor until it forms a ball. Slowly increase the speed until the ball falls apart and sticks to the sides of the bowl. Remove the cheese from the bowl with a rubber spatula, and press it tightly into an old-fashioned cheese crock.

3. Cut a piece of white paper exactly to the size of the opening of the cheese crock. Dip the paper into the liquor used in the cheese; then place it on the cheese, and press it firmly down. Be sure no air pocket remains. Close the lid tightly on the pot and refrigerate. The cheese will keep in the refrigerator for 6 months to 1 year.

Yields 1 pound.

Butter making is no chore, according to this picture showing a Tillinghast centrifugal churn that won first prize at the industrial exhibit at the Crystal Palace in 1843.

DR. SAMUEL H. MOFFETT, INVENTOR OF THE BELL REGISTER.

[FROM A PHOTOGRAPH BY ANDERSON, RICHMOND, VA.]

The Moffett bell register was an ingenious device that recorded amount of liquor consumed in a tavern, thereby permitting the state to claim the taxes due on consumption.

A scene from a San Francisco Chinese restaurant, where chop suey and chow mein originated.

KITCHEN PEPPER

Directions for Cookery

By Eliza Leslie

Every good cook attempts to establish a "taste identity" for her or his cooking. From the earliest times, good cooks and chefs always made their own spice mixtures, which they used in literally every dish. These mixtures did not dull or make uniform the taste of their food, but rather they brought to a peak the taste of everything, be it lamb, poultry, beef, pork, or vegetables.

This kitchen pepper recipe is very American, mixing together several Old World spices with a few known only since the discovery of the Western Hemisphere.

It is very important to make this mixture in small quantities. Even the small quantity given here is better divided into two or three very small portions and kept in tiny well-sealed glass containers to retain freshness.

INGREDIENTS:

8 tablespoons white powdered ginger

2 tablespoons plus 2 teaspoons black pepper

4 tablespoons white Montauk pepper

4 tablespoons ground cinnamon

4 tablespoons ground nutmeg

1 tablespoon plus 1 teaspoon ground cloves

METHOD:

1. Measure out the ingredients, placing them in a small bowl.
2. Gently stir until mixed. Sift the mixture two or three times through a fine sieve in order to blend the ingredients perfectly.
3. Divide it into three small amounts and put each into a small glass jar and close it with a cork or plastic stopper.

Yields 2 cups.

Benjamin Thompson, a Yankee by birth, was dubbed Count Rumford by the king of Bavaria. His invention of a stove won him the honor.

ORANGE FOOL

Home Cookery: A Collection of Tested Recipes

By Mrs. Chadwick

As for its ingredients, this recipe is international, and it could be from any part of the world. What makes it American is the method, the speed of preparation, and the convenience of using one single container from the beginning of the preparation to the end of cooking.

INGREDIENTS:

6 large eggs

½ cup sugar

⅛ teaspoon cinnamon

⅛ teaspoon nutmeg

2 cups light cream (half-and-half)

juice of 6 ripe oranges or 3 cups fresh frozen orange juice

2 tablespoons butter (¼ stick)

whipped cream, grated orange peel, or slice of orange for garnish

METHOD:

1. In the top of a double boiler, beat the eggs with a hand beater until they turn frothy and lemon yellow.
2. Beat in the sugar and spices.
3. Beat in the cream.
4. Add the juice in small quantities, beating it constantly.
5. Place the mixture over boiling water into the double boiler, and adjust the heat so that the water stops boiling and just simmers. Keep beating with the hand beater until mixture thickens enough to coat the spoon when dipped into the mixture.

6.   Add the butter; remove from the heat, and keep beating for another minute or two.

7.   Place the top part of the double boiler in ice water, beat the mixture for a few seconds every 2 or 3 minutes, until it cools and gets even thicker.

8.   Refrigerate in a serving dish or spoon it out into six glass serving dishes or shallow champagne or wine glasses. Serve cold. Decorate the top, if you wish, with a small dab of whipped cream, some grated orange peel, or an orange slice.

Serves 6.

"Le Garçon de Cafe," French cartoon, undated.

WILD PLUM CATSUP

Presbyterian Cook Book

Compiled by the Ladies of the First Presbyterian Church

Dayton, Ohio

Wild plums or beach plums, a native American fruit, were once available in all markets, and can still be found occasionally in supermarkets. If neither is available, use the so-called Italian plums, which are relatively inexpensive and in great abundance for a few weeks in September.

This catsup makes a beautiful gift. As a sauce, it elevates plain broiled chops, chicken, and other everyday dishes to the level of American gourmet.

INGREDIENTS:

10 pounds plums

5 pounds sugar

1 quart plain white vinegar

1 teaspoon ground cinnamon

½ teaspoon ground nutmeg

½ teaspoon ground cloves

METHOD:

1. Wash and shake dry the plums; discard the stems. Do not pit.
2. Add the sugar to the washed plums, and place the container with the lid tightly closed over medium heat. After 30 minutes, increase the heat, and stir the plum-sugar mixture. Break some of the plums with the wooden spoon.
3. Continue the cooking, stirring the mixture occasionally so that it does not stick to the bottom. In approximately 15 minutes, all the plums will be cooked through and mashed.

4.   Remove from the fire and cool.

5.   Mash the mixture with a wooden spoon. Put the mashed pulp through a fine sieve, and continue mashing until all the liquid and some of the pulp goes through. Discard the pits and the skins. There should be approximately 4 quarts of liquid.

6.   Boil the vinegar together with the spices for a few minutes.

7.   Add the vinegar spice mixture to the plum liquid, then boil vigorously, stirring constantly, for 15 minutes, or until the liquid has reduced to 4 quarts again.

8.   Place the empty bottles, which have been washed and boiled, on a cookie sheet or in a large metal pan. Use a metal funnel, if possible, to pour the hot catsup into the bottles; this will prevent the bottles from cracking.

9.   Let the catsup cool; close the bottles, and let it stand at room temperature overnight. Refrigerate. After two days, remove from the refrigerator and store in a cool place without sunshine. The catsup will keep for several years.

Yields 8 pint bottles.

TOGUS BREAD

The Kansas Home Cook Book

Compiled by Cushing and Gray

The presence of corn meal, still called Indian meal, and molasses are proof enough of the Yankee origin of this bread.

INGREDIENTS:

3 cups milk

1 cup sour cream

1 cup molasses

1 cup all-purpose flour

1 teaspoon baking powder

1 teaspoon salt

3 cups medium-grind yellow corn meal

METHOD:

1. Preheat the oven to 400 degrees.
2. Rinse two large empty juice or coffee cans from which the tops have been carefully cut off with a good sharp can opener so that no rough edges remain. Dry the inside of the cans, and brush them lightly with some oil or butter.
3. In the bowl of an electric mixer, slowly add the sour cream and the molasses to the milk. Mix on the lowest speed.
4. Sift the salt and baking powder into the one cup of flour; then gently add the flour mixture to the corn meal. Still on slow speed, add the dry ingredients to the liquid ingredients.
5. Divide it between the two cans.

6.   In the meantime, bring enough water to a boil in a large pot to cover two-thirds of the submerged cans. Place the cans in the boiling water; cover the pot with a lid, and bring to a boil again. When it boils, place it in the oven, and steam the bread for approximately 3 hours.

7.   Let the bread cool in the can. When cool, remove the bottom of the can. Run the edge of a sharp knife around the inside, and remove the Togus Bread. It can be eaten warm, cold, or toasted.

Yields 2 round loaves, each 8 slices.

Farina mill as pictured in a travel book on America, 1671.

APPLEADE

Mrs. Porter's New Southern Cookery Book

By Mrs. M. E. Porter

This recipe dates back to colonial times, and it is an interesting variation on today's artificially flavored soft drinks.

INGREDIENTS:

6 medium-sized apples (practically any kind will do)
2 quarts boiling water
½ to ¾ cup sugar, depending on the sweetness of the apples
2 pieces of lemon peel, approximately 2 inches long and one inch wide
juice of one large lemon (about ⅓ cup fresh lemon juice)

METHOD:

1. Slice the apples, including the skin and core. Do not discard any part. Lay the slices in a deep pot with a tight-fitting lid.
2. Pour the boiling water over the apple slices. Cover immediately with the lid, and let it stand for two to three hours. Refrigerate overnight.
3. Strain the juice through a fine sieve. Press the apples gently, taking care that no pulp goes into the clear liquid.
4. Add the lemon peel and the lemon juice to the liquid, then stir in sugar to taste.
5. Fill one ice cube tray with the liquid and freeze it; chill the rest. Serve the appleade with appleade ice cubes in it.

Yields 2 quarts.

COLD COMPOTE

Handbook of Practical Cookery for Ladies and Professional Cooks

By Pierre Blot

This dish is uniquely American because of one ingredient—the maple syrup. The combination of the syrup and red currant jelly makes a simple and beautiful dessert.

INGREDIENTS:

1 pint basket of small or medium-sized ripe strawberries

1 pint of fresh raspberries

1 cup real maple syrup or maple-flavored syrup

1 cup red currant jelly

green leaves for garnish

METHOD:

1. Quickly wash the strawberries under running tepid water in a colander. Move your spread-out fingers above them so the water does not hit the berries but dribbles through your fingers.
2. Gently pat the side of the colander and spread the berries on a kitchen towel or absorbent paper.
3. Repeat the same procedure with the raspberries, drying them as gently as possible to avoid bruising them.
4. Hull all the strawberries except one or two that have the greenest top parts and the longest, freshest stems. Set these aside for decoration.
5. Arrange the berries on a serving dish and chill.

ing tropical fruits at Burling Slip, New York, ca. 1880.

6. In a small container, boil together the syrup and jelly, stirring constantly until all lumps disappear and the mixture comes to a gentle boil.

7. Let it cool for 1-2 minutes, then gently spoon the hot mixture over the berries, starting always on the top to coat them as evenly as possible.

8. Chill again, for at least 1 hour. Decorate the top with the unhulled berries arranged on top of the leaves, and serve.

Serves 4.

Early advertisement for William M. Stedman & Company, wholesale grocers in Boston, 1880s.

VEAL LOAF

Capitol City Cook Book

By the Grace Church Women's Guild

This, again, is a dish that is very American because of the method of preparation rather than the ingredients. It is not as elaborate as Old World meat loaves, and it takes advantage of modern methods and ingredients, such as the electric beater and cracker meal. It is a very good dish hot, but is especially excellent cold. Try it with the Wild Plum Catsup.

INGREDIENTS:

3 pounds ground veal

½ pound ground pork

3 well-beaten eggs

1 tablespoon salt

1 tablespoon powdered sage

1 teaspoon black pepper

10 tablespoons cracker meal

or

the same amount of rolled Saltines

4 tablespoons (½ stick) butter dissolved in 2 cups boiling water

METHOD:

1. Brush the inside of a 3-quart loaf pan with some lard, oil, or bacon grease. Preheat the oven to 325 degrees.
2. By hand, mix all the spices into the pork.
3. Beat the eggs with an electric beater until they turn frothy and lemon colored.

4. Wet hands, and mix the ground veal thoroughly with the eggs. Work in the pork-spice mixture until evenly distributed.

5. Sprinkle the cracker meal or rolled crackers on the meat, and work in.

6. Pour in the now-cooled water and butter mixture in small quantities, working it into the meat as it is added.

7. Press the mixture into the loaf pan. Bake for 2½ to 3 hours.

Yields 8 generous dinner servings, and even more cold sliced loaf.

The St. Ghistlain pear, imported from Belgium, became one of the favorite crops on American fruit farms in the 1830s.

ST. GHISTLAIN PEAR.

PICKLED CHICKEN

The Kansas Home Cook Book

By Mrs. L. G. Raymond, compiled by Cushing and Gray

In Europe, there was a saying that farmers eat chicken only in time of sickness. That means if either the farmer or the chicken is sick. Not so in the United States. On the early American farms, chicken was a staple and was cooked in many, many forms and ways. This recipe is one of the unique methods developed in the Missouri and Kansas farmlands.

INGREDIENTS:

1 fowl, approximately 4 to 5 pounds, cut into 4 pieces

1 small onion, split in half

1 cup sliced carrots

2 cloves of garlic

10 peppercorns

1 stalk of celery

3 sprigs of parsley

1 bay leaf

1 tablespoon salt

enough water to cover the chicken plus 2 inches extra

1 pint vinegar

1 teaspoon sugar

juice of one lemon

parsley and lemon for garnish

METHOD:

1. Put the chicken and all except the last four ingredients in a deep pot with a good lid. Bring to a boil over medium heat, and then adjust the heat to low, simmering for 3 to 4 hours, or until the bone slides out from the meat easily when picked up.

2. Remove from the fire; strain the liquid through a fine sieve and then through a double-folded wet kitchen cloth placed in the sieve. Refrigerate the liquid.

3. Remove and discard all bones and cartilage, and cut the fowl into bite-sized pieces.

4. Bring the vinegar and the sugar to a boil in a small pot. Remove from the heat and pour it over the chicken pieces.

5. Take the liquid out of the refrigerator, and skim off all the fat that has congealed on the top of it. Pour the liquid over the chicken, and stir so that it mixes with the hot vinegar.

6. Add the lemon juice; cool to room temperature; then chill.

7. Serve it in thin slices decorated with fresh parsley and tiny lemon wedges.

Serves 8 for lunch.

Weighing and packing halibut, Gloucester, unda

ESCABECHE

High Living

Compiled by L. L. McLaren

This old, native Peruvian recipe came to California during the Spanish occupation, and became, in its refined form, a part of Californian cuisine.

INGREDIENTS:

2 pounds filet of pike, grouper, swordfish, halibut,
or any other firm white fish

3 tablespoons oil

1 tablespoon vinegar

1 teaspoon salt

1/8 teaspoon cayenne pepper

a 2-inch by 1-inch orange peel, thin, if possible, and without the
white pulp inside, cut into pieces resembling shredded coconut

1 teaspoon onion juice or 2 teaspoons grated onion

2 whole fresh bay leaves, washed and broken into 4 or 5 pieces

sprig of fresh thyme or 1/4 teaspoon dry thyme

1 cup very thin slices green pepper (bell pepper, cubinello or
sweet banana pepper)

1 large orange peeled and sliced crosswise

4 to 6 large lettuce leaves

METHOD:

1. With a wire whisk mix vigorously the oil, vinegar, salt, cayenne pepper, orange peel, onion juice, bay leaves, and thyme.
2. Cut the fish into finger thick pieces; plunge into one quart boiling water with one tablespoon salt. Let the water come back to boil again over medium heat. Remove from heat, and let it stand for 10 minutes. Pour off the liquid; discard.

143

3. Gently mix the fish with the green pepper slices. Pour the oil-vinegar-spice mixture over the fish. Refrigerate for 1 to 3 hours. Gently stir it every hour so that the marinade coats all the pieces.
4. Line a salad bowl with lettuce leaves. Pile the fish mixture in the middle, and decorate it with the thin orange slices.

Serves 8.

Advertisement for a stove

144

TOMATO CURRY

Cooking in Old Creole Days

By Celestine Eustis

Some of the Creole dishes originated in France and were brought by the French settlers to New Orleans; others came from Spain, and some, such as the recipe below, were originally developed in the southern Louisiana surroundings and do not have a counterpart in either the old French or the old Spanish cuisine.

INGREDIENTS:

1 large can peeled whole tomatoes

1 teaspoon sugar

½ teaspoon salt

1 tablespoon curry powder

⅛ teaspoon cayenne pepper

1 cup white bread crumbs

1 cup uncooked, washed Louisiana rice

4 tablespoons butter (½ stick)

1 tablespoon chopped fresh parsley

METHOD:

1. Preheat the oven to 300 degrees.
2. Mix the sugar and spices with the tomatoes with a large spoon, gently breaking the tomatoes into small chunks with the edge of the spoon.
3. Butter the bottom and sides of a 2 quart ovenproof casserole with one tablespoon of the butter and lightly sprinkle the bottom with some of the bread crumbs.
4. Sprinkle ⅓ cup rice on the crumbs and spoon over it ⅓ of the tomato mixture. Repeat this two more times, until all rice and tomato is used.

5. Melt the butter in a frying pan and gently toast the bread crumbs in it. Cover the top layer of tomatoes with the bread crumbs.

6. Cover and bake the casserole for 45 minutes. Bake uncovered for an additional 15 minutes.

7. Sprinkle with the freshly chopped parsley and serve as a side dish with meat. It is especially good with pork chops, veal chops, or roast veal.

Serves 8.

Advertisement for an inn called the Madison Cottage, ca. 1860-1

JUMBALLAYA A LA CREOLE

Cooking in Old Creole Days

By Celestine Eustis

If you consulted a dictionary—or even read an old recipe for this dish—you would conclude that the word *jumballaya* means a heap of things thrown together. But when you sit down and eat this food, you will have to agree that it was thrown together by a culinary genius. After making Jumballaya à la Creole a few times, you may decide to become inventive—omitting or adding ingredients according to your taste.

INGREDIENTS:

1 cup rice

6 cups water

2 ¾ teaspoons salt

1 chicken, 2 to 2 ½ pounds, cut into 8 pieces

6 tablespoons flour

¾ teaspoon black pepper

1 tablespoon minced or grated onion

4 tablespoons oil

1 bay leaf

1 small can (8 ounce size) broken tomato pieces

or

1 small can whole tomatoes

½ teaspoon Tabasco sauce

½ teaspoon plus 1 tablespoon sugar

⅛ teaspoon garlic salt

4 tablespoons butter

2 tablespoons oil
1 can okra, drained and rinsed
1 cup frozen peas
1 small can minced clams
½ pound Italian sausage
or
½ pound breakfast sausage
4 to 6 tablespoons parsley, coarsely chopped

METHOD:

1.   In a large pan, cook the rice and 1 teaspoon salt in 3 cups of water for 5 minutes. Remove from the stove; strain, and discard the liquid. Place the rice back in the pot in which it cooked, and set aside.

2.   Mix 4 tablespoons flour with 1 teaspoon salt and ½ teaspoon pepper. Dredge the chicken pieces until they are evenly coated.

3.   In a frying pan, heat the oil until it smokes. Fry the chicken pieces, turning them until they are deep brown on all sides. Remove to a plate and keep warm.

4.   Add the minced onion, bay leaf, and 2 tablespoons remaining flour to the pan in which the chicken was cooked. Stir the mixture until it starts to brown, then remove from the stove, and briskly stir in 1 cup of water. Bring to a boil, stirring constantly. After 2 to 3 minutes of boiling, strain the sauce into a small bowl. Immediately return the chicken to the pan. Strain the sauce over the chicken, and add the remaining two cups of water. Cover the pot; bring to a boil; then reduce the heat, and simmer for 30 minutes.

5.   After 30 minutes, check the sauce for color. If it is not brown enough, add a teaspoon of Kitchen Bouquet. Then add the chicken and sauce to the rice. Cover the pan loosely with aluminum foil, and cook over slow heat for 10 minutes, stirring occasionally with a fork to prevent sticking. Reduce heat and keep warm while you make the sauce.

6.   In the same pot in which the chicken was cooked, bring the tomatoes in their liquid, ¼ teaspoon salt, ¼ teaspoon pepper, ½ teaspoon sugar, and garlic salt to a boil. Add 2 tablespoons butter and stir. Add this mixture to the chicken-rice mixture.

7.   Place 2 tablespoons butter, 1 tablespoon sugar, ½ teaspoon salt in the same pan in which the tomatoes were cooked. When the butter has melted, add the frozen peas. Cover and steam for 5 minutes. Then pour this mixture over the chicken-rice-tomato mixture.

8.   Strain the minced clams, saving the liquid. Add the clams to the main mixture, and fold in with a fork, scraping the bottom as you work. If the mixture seems too dry, add some or all of the clam juice.

9.   Place the cold sausage into a cold frying pan. Prick with a fork on all sides. Turn the heat to medium. Sprinkle the sausage with 2 to 3 tablespoons water; cover, and cook slowly for about 20 minutes for breakfast sausage, 30 minutes for Italian sausage. Remove the lid; increase the heat to make the water evaporate, and brown the sausages on all sides. Break it into bite-sized pieces. Discard the fat, and gently fold the sausage pieces into the jumballaya. Correct the seasoning, add 1 to 3 tablespoons parsley, more salt or Tabasco to taste. Sprinkle the top with 2 to 3 tablespoons more parsley as garnish. Serve the jumballaya piping hot in a very large dish. This dish is good with hot French bread, and a good red wine, beer, or mint juleps.

Serves 8 hungry men or 12 people.

A WOODMAN BEGINNING A CLEARING.

Illustration from an article about the American frontier, The Christian Weekly, *undated.*

NINE-DAY PICKLES

Dorcus Cook Book

Published by the Dorcus Society of St. John Lutheran Church

Although it is hard to prove the American origin of this recipe, I have never found anything like it in my several hundred European books on pickling. Many are similar, but this is, in my opinion, one of the easiest to prepare and the best to eat.

INGREDIENTS FOR BRINE:
7 pounds cucumbers

1 gallon water

2 cups salt

1 quart vinegar

1 tablespoon alum (available from pharmacist)

INGREDIENTS FOR SYRUP:
6 cups vinegar

3½ pounds sugar plus 2 cups

4 tablespoons allspice

2 tablespoons celery seeds

4 cinnamon sticks, 2½ to 3 inches each

METHOD:

1. Wash and dry cucumbers; cut off the ends, and cut them into pieces 2½ by 3 inches.
2. Bring 1 gallon of water to a boil. When it boils, stir in 2 cups of salt. Remove from the fire and let cool.
3. Place the cucumbers in this mixture; refrigerate for 3 days.

4. Discard the liquid. Place the cucumbers in 1 gallon of fresh water. Store the cucumbers for 3 days, changing the water each day.

5. On the fourth day, remove the cucumbers and cut them crosswise into 1-inch pieces. Bring the water, vinegar, and alum to a boil. Add the cucumbers, and simmer gently for 2 hours. Do not let the cucumbers boil.

6. To make the syrup, boil together vinegar with 3½ pounds sugar, the allspice, celery seed, and the cinnamon.

7. Distribute cucumber pieces in six or eight pickling jars. Pour the vinegar syrup over the jars, dividing equally.

8. For 3 days, each morning pour off syrup; reheat to boiling point, and pour back over the pickles.

9. On the last day, the ninth, add 2 cups sugar to the reboiling syrup before pouring back into jars.

Yields 6 to 8 jars.

GIRL SCOUT DRUMSTICKS

Dorcus Cook Book

Published by Dorcus Society of St. John Lutheran Church

If any food is more American than apple pie, it is probably corn-flakes. Although it was originally invented strictly as a convenience breakfast food, the ingenuity of the American homemaker has made it into one of the most important ingredients in American cooking. This dish is a tasty way to use America's number one in-gredient.

INGREDIENTS:

1 pound ground beef

2 ice cubes, crushed

2 tablespoons chopped onion

½ teaspoon salt

light sprinkling black pepper

1 egg

1 cup cornflakes

METHOD:

1. Break ground meat into small parts in a large mixing bowl. Add crushed ice, chopped onions, salt and pepper, and the un-beaten egg.
2. With wet hands, work the ice cubes, egg, onion, salt, and pep-per into the meat until all ice disappears and mixture is moist and smooth.
3. Sprinkle the cornflakes on top of the meat, and work them into the mixture quickly and lightly so they are not crushed.
4. Divide the mixture into 8 equal parts, and with wet hands, form into 8 sausage-shaped portions. Refrigerate for 2 to 3 hours.

5. Clean the bark from eight 14-18″ long, thin branches, and cut the barkless end to a point. Carefully position each stick into a drumstick. Roast over a campfire.

6. Remove from stick into a hot dog bun and serve with catsup or chili sauce.

Yields 8 drumsticks.

A banana warehouse, New York, illustration from a periodical, ca. 1850-187

BEEFSTEAK AND BANANAS

Y.M.C.A. Cook Book

Compiled by the Young Men's Christian Association

Bananas, native to the North and South American continents, are one of the most American of all fruits. In the United States they are eaten mainly as fruit, but the natives used them in many forms as a staple. In this recipe, they accompany a beefsteak, and they certainly give a unique taste combination and interesting appearance.

INGREDIENTS:

6-8 firm, not-too-ripe bananas

4 teaspoons sugar

1 teaspoon butter

1 teaspoon lemon juice

8 top sirloin or sirloin steaks, 12 ounces each

1 tablespoon salt mixed with ½ teaspoon black pepper

⅛ teaspoon garlic salt

⅛ teaspoon paprika

1 tablespoon Kitchen Bouquet

4 tablespoons shortening:
½ butter and ½ oil
or ½ lard and ½ oil

parsley for garnish

METHOD:

1. Preheat the oven to 300 degrees.
2. Peel bananas; cut in half; split each half into 2 long pieces. Place in an ovenproof serving dish or in a baking dish.
3. In a small saucepan, melt butter and stir in sugar and lemon juice.

155

4. Sprinkle the mixture over the bananas. Bake for approximately 20 minutes.

5. In the meantime, wrap both sides of each steak with the spices and brush both sides with the Kitchen Bouquet.

6. Over high heat, heat the butter-oil mixture until it is very hot. Place 4 steaks in the hot pan, cook for 1 minute and remove. Let the pan recover the lost heat for 3 to 4 minutes. Repeat the same procedure with other side of the 4 steaks, then let the pan stay empty over high heat again. Repeat this procedure with other steaks. Then pan-fry the steaks, four at a time, for a total of 10 to 12 minutes for medium-rare, turning them every 3 to 4 minutes. Keep them warm until all 8 steaks are done.

7. Serve steaks surrounded with bananas decorated with parsley.

Serves 8.

Shipping watermelons by rail from Atlanta, Geor

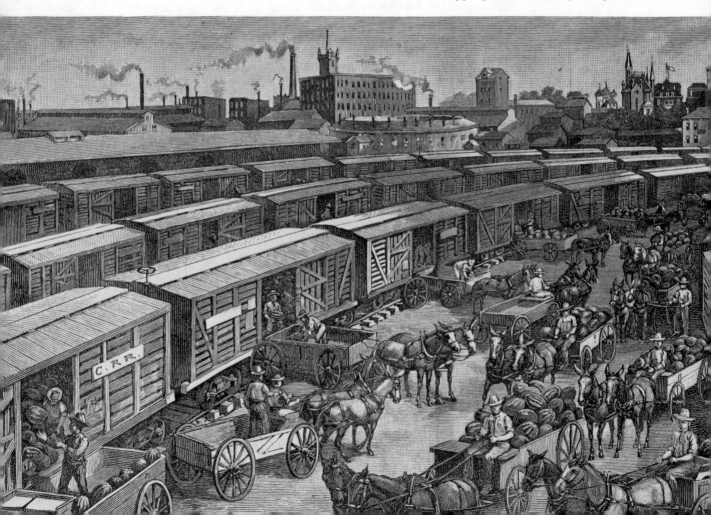

Notes

American Foods

Page 16

1. Mrs. Chadwick's *Home Cookery* (1853), page 102, "Alamode Beef": "Take a nice piece of rump of beef weighing about twelve pounds..."

2. *Ibid.,* pages 82 and 83, "Real Turtle Soup": "....This makes four or five tureens of soup."

3. Mrs. Porter's *New Southern Cookery Book* (1871), page 266, "Lady Cake": "One pound and a quarter of butter, one pound and a quarter of sugar, one pound and a half of flour, the whites of twenty eggs..."

4. For example, see the second volume of the Arno Press reprint series of **American Gastronomy:** *Directions for Cookery in Its Various Branches* (1848) by Miss Leslie. It is reprinted for the series from the 31st edition.

Page 17

5. Columbus brought home turkey ("Indian hen") eggs on his

second voyage. They were hatched by hens and ducks; raised carefully; and became very popular throughout the Old World. In 1687, M. Marxen Rumpolt, chief cook to one of the ruling princes of the Holy Empire, included in his book, *Ein Neu Kochbuch Das ist ein Gruendtliche Beschreibung* (1587), twenty-two recipes on how to prepare Indian hen.

Page 18
6. *The Martha Washington Cook Book* (1940) by Marie Kimball, page 32.

Page 24
7. A "pizza" does exist in Italy—it is a flat bread, sometimes brushed with tomato paste, baked at home on bread-baking day.

American Cooks and Chefs

Page 36
1. "Visit to a Negro Cabin in Virginia," published in the *Family Magazine,* December, 1835.

Page 38
2. *The Kansas Home Cook Book* (1886), compiled by Mrs. C. H. Cushing and Mrs. B. Gray, published by the Board of Managers for the Benefit of the Home for the Friendless, Leavenworth, Kansas, reprinted by Arno Press, Inc., New York, 1973.

American Dishes

Page 44
1. *Ein Neu Kochbuch Das ist ein Gruendtliche Beschreibung* (1587), page 144, recipe 37.

Metric Recipe Conversions

These conversions are based on the liter measure, which is widely used throughout Europe for liquid and dry measures. Because there are no metric measuring devices that are equivalent to the American teaspoon and tablespoon, these measurements have been retained.

TO FRICASSEE A SMALL CHICKEN, SOUTHERN MODE
Page 57

4 small spring chickens, 1.4 to 1.6 kilograms

1 ½ tablespoons salt

½ teaspoon black pepper

¼ teaspoon mace

enough water to cover

.25 liter of the cooking liquid

6 tablespoons butter (¾ stick)

2 tablespoons flour

.25 liter plus 3 tablespoons milk

8 tablespoons white wine

WONDERS OR CRULLERS
Page 61

.5 liter flour

1.18 liter granulated sugar

½ teaspoon ground nutmeg

8 tablespoons butter (1 stick)

3 eggs, slightly beaten

1 tablespoon rum (or rose water, if available)

.125 liter sifted flour, for dusting

.5 liter oil combined with 1 liter lard
or
other shortening for frying
powdered sugar

STEWED FROG LEGS
Page 63

4 tablespoons butter (½ stick)

16 pairs large, or 24 pairs medium-sized, fresh or frozen frog hind legs,
skinned and blanched

1 teaspoon flour

¼ teaspoon dry thyme

pinch of white pepper and salt to taste

2 sprigs parsley

1 bay leaf

2 whole cloves, slightly bruised

1 clove garlic, mashed to a pulp with ½ teaspoon salt

1.25 liter dry white wine

2 egg yolks

parsley sprigs, watercress, and lemon wedges for garnish, optional

SWEET POTATO PUDDING
Page 67

5 eggs
8 tablespoons butter (1 stick)
1.125 liter sugar
1 can, 454-gram size, sweet potatoes or whole yams
1 lemon
whipped cream or a tart fruit sauce, optional

SAUSAGES
Page 69

1.6 kilogram lean pork shoulder
1.6 kilogram lean boneless pork loin
1 tablespoon salt
½ teaspoon ground black pepper
¼ teaspoon ground white pepper
1 teaspoon rubbed (powdered) sage
¼ teaspoon powdered basil
1 pinch garlic salt
.25 liter lukewarm water
.06 liter sifted flour

PEACH SAUCE
Page 73

1 package, 454-gram size, dried peaches
.5 liter hot water
.25 liter brown sugar

MISSISSIPPI CORN BREAD
Page 75

8 tablespoons butter (½ stick)
454 grams cornmeal
1 teaspoon salt
.5 liter buttermilk, mixed with 1 teaspoon baking soda

MEXICAN EGGS
Page 77

2 tablespoons butter or bacon drippings
2 tablespoons finely chopped bell pepper
2 tablespoons finely chopped onion
1 can, 454-gram size, stewed tomatoes, drained
(liquid can be saved for later use)
½ teaspoon salt
.125 liter milk or light cream beaten into 16 eggs
Tabasco sauce, optional

DRESDEN DRESSING
Page 79

3 hard-boiled eggs
.125 liter finely grated or finely minced onion
2 tablespoons chopped green parsley
1 scant teaspoon salt
1 scant teaspoon sugar
1 pinch dry mustard
.06 liter corn oil
.06 liter white vinegar

BOILED FOWL
Page 83

1 stewing hen or a young fowl, 2 to 2.5 kilograms

salt and white pepper, according to taste

¼ teaspoon garlic salt, optional

4 tablespoons butter (½ stick)

2 dozen shucked oysters

1 tablespoon flour

.25 liter light cream or milk

1 tablespoon chopped fresh green parsley

HASHED LITTLE NECK CLAMS
ON TOAST
Page 85

4 tablespoons butter (½ stick)

2 cans, 228-gram size, minced clams

1 teaspoon freshly chopped green parsley

1 teaspoon freshly chopped chives or ¼ teaspoon dried chives

salt and freshly ground black pepper, according to taste

.08 liter dry white bread crumbs, made from
Italian or French bread

.06 liter sherry

8 slices toast, buttered or plain

SWEET POTATO WAFFLES
Page 87

.5 liter mashed, boiled sweet potatoes
2 eggs, separated
.125 liter granulated sugar
.25 liter melted, warm butter
.5 liter milk
4 to 6 tablespoons flour
shortening to brush waffle iron

SWEET POTATO BUNS
Page 89

3 tablespoons lukewarm water
1 package dry yeast
pinch of sugar
1 can, .6-kilogram size, yams, rinsed and patted dry
.25 liter sifted flour
4 tablespoons butter, at room temperature
additional flour for dusting

HAM AND SWEET POTATO SALAD
Page 91

.5 liter diced, cooked ham, cut into 1 centimeter cubes
.5 liter diced, cooked sweet potato, cut into 1 centimeter cubes
.25 liter diced celery, cut in 5 millimeter dice
.25 liter apple, cut in 5 millimeter dice
.25 liter fresh orange sections
.06 liter chopped pecans (optional)
.25 liter mayonnaise

POTATO DRESSING
Page 93

1 boiled, medium-sized potato, still warm

2 egg yolks, hard-boiled

1 teaspoon butter

½ teaspoon prepared mustard

salt, according to taste

.125 liter white vinegar

.25 liter corn oil or olive oil

2 teaspoons sugar

1 tablespoon lemon juice

few drops onion juice

Tabasco sauce, according to taste

GRAPEFRUIT AND LOBSTER SALAD
Page 95

4 large grapefruits

2 lobsters, .6 to .9 kilograms, or lobster tails, 200 to 230 grams each

.125 cup finely minced celery, if possible, the hearts

2 tablespoons finely chopped pecans

.25 liter mayonnaise-type salad dressing

or

the same amount of homemade mayonnaise

1 bunch watercress

OYSTER SHORTCAKE
Page 97

INGREDIENTS FOR CRUST:

.5 liter flour

2 teaspoons baking powder

½ teaspoon salt

.18 liter milk, at room temperature

2 tablespoons melted butter

INGREDIENTS FOR FILLING:

.5 liter shucked oysters, or equivalent in canned oysters

2 tablespoons water

3 tablespoons butter

3 tablespoons flour

.37 liter milk

salt and freshly ground black pepper, according to taste

PEANUT BRITTLE DESSERT
Page 101

20 marshmallows

.125 liter heavy cream

.18 liter peanut brittle, ground or finely chopped

TOMATO MARMALADE
Page 103

*12 medium-sized tomatoes, approximately 6 centimeters in diameter
and 4 to 5 centimeters high, ripened but still firm*

2 small, thin-skinned lemons

.5 liter sugar

.9 liter boiling water

ROUND STEAK SAUSAGE FORCEMEAT
Page 105

2 round steaks, 454 grams each, well trimmed and as lean as possible
(save trimmings)
salt and freshly ground black pepper to taste
454 grams bulk pork sausage
.25 liter white bread crumbs, tightly packed
2 tablespoons flour
2 to 3 tablespoons bacon drippings, plus all fat trimmings from the steaks
.25 to .5 liter soup stock, canned consommé, or water
8 to 10 medium-sized potatoes, peeled and halved

APPLE CATSUP
Page 109

12 large, firm, tart apples
.25 liter sugar
1 teaspoon white pepper
1 teaspoon ground cloves
1 teaspoon dry mustard
2 medium-sized white onions, finely minced
.5 liter white pickling vinegar
2 teaspoons cinnamon
1 tablespoon salt
.125 liter prepared horseradish

BAKED STUFFED POTATOES
Page 111

8 large, round potatoes, 5 to 6 centimeters in diameter

2 slices of bacon, cut in 5 millimeter pieces

3 tablespoons finely chopped onions

3 tablespoons finely chopped celery

salt and freshly ground black pepper to taste

454 grams ground beef

.25 liter milk

.5 liter boiling water

1 teaspoon flour dissolved in an additional .125 liter milk

chopped parsley, optional

CHILI
Page 113

227 grams salt pork

1.25 to 1.5 liters water

1 can, 298-gram size, cream of tomato soup

1.5 liters chili beans (or, if not available, use a No. 2 can, .37 liter, kidney beans with 1 teaspoon chili powder added)

½ clove garlic

2 teaspoons cumin seeds

908 grams round steak or similar cut

salt, according to taste

additional chili powder to taste

flour to dredge meat and onions

3 to 4 medium-sized onions

1 to 2 red bell peppers

BUTTERSCOTCH CAKE PUDDING
Page 115

INGREDIENTS FOR THE SYRUP:
.25 liter brown sugar
1 tablespoon butter
.45 liter boiling water

INGREDIENTS FOR THE CAKE:
.25 liter sugar
1 tablespoon butter, room temperature
.25 liter flour
2 teaspoons baking powder
.125 liter milk
1 teaspoon cinnamon, optional
½ teaspoon nutmeg, optional
.125 liter raisins, optional
whipped cream, optional

WILD ONIONS AND EGGS
Page 119

2 bunches wild onions, 10 to 12 in each bunch
4 slices ranch-style bacon, thickly sliced, cut into 1 centimeter strips
2 tablespoons water
8 eggs
.125 liter milk
salt and freshly ground black pepper, according to taste

BURNT SUGAR CAKE
Page 121

INGREDIENTS FOR BURNT SUGAR:

.25 liter sugar

.25 liter water

INGREDIENTS FOR THE CAKE:

.5 liter sugar

.25 liter butter

4 egg yolks, lightly beaten

1.25 liter flour

3 teaspoonsful baking powder

.5 liter water

few drops of vanilla

.06 liter burnt sugar (or more, depending on taste)

TO POT CHEESE
Page 123

454 grams soft or semi-soft cheese, such as Port Salut

1 tablespoon brandy or good bourbon

KITCHEN PEPPER
Page 127

No metric conversion required.

ORANGE FOOL
Page 129

6 large eggs
.125 liter sugar
⅛ teaspoon cinnamon
⅛ teaspoon nutmeg
.5 liter light cream (half-and-half)
juice of 6 ripe oranges or ¾ liter fresh, frozen orange juice
2 tablespoons butter (¼ stick)
whipped cream, grated orange peel, or slice of orange for garnish

WILD PLUM CATSUP
Page 131

4.5 kilograms plums
2.3 kilograms sugar
.9 liter plain white vinegar
1 teaspoon ground cinnamon
½ teaspoon ground nutmeg
½ teaspoon ground cloves

TOGUS BREAD
Page 133

.75 liter milk
.25 liter sour cream
.25 liter molasses
.25 liter all-purpose flour
1 teaspoon baking powder
1 teaspoon salt
.75 liter medium-grind yellow corn meal

APPLEADE
Page 135

6 medium-sized apples (practically any kind will do)

1.9 liters boiling water

.125 liter sugar, depending on the sweetness of the apples

*2 pieces of lemon peel, approximately 5 centimeters long and
2.5 centimeters wide*

juice of one large lemon (about .08 liter fresh lemon juice)

COLD COMPOTE
Page 137

.5 liter small or medium-sized ripe strawberries

.5 liter fresh raspberries

.125 liter real maple syrup or maple-flavored syrup

.25 liter red currant jelly

green leaves for garnish

VEAL LOAF
Page 139

1.4 kilograms ground veal

.2 kilograms ground pork

3 well-beaten eggs

1 tablespoon salt

1 tablespoon powdered sage

1 teaspoon black pepper

10 tablespoons cracker meal

or

the same amount of rolled Saltines

4 tablespoons (½ stick) butter dissolved in ½ liter boiling water

PICKLED CHICKEN
Page 141

1 fowl, approximately 1.8 to 2 kilograms, cut into 4 pieces

1 small onion, split in half

.25 liter sliced carrot

2 cloves of garlic

10 peppercorns

1 stalk of celery

3 sprigs of parsley

1 bay leaf

1 tablespoon salt

enough water to cover the chicken plus 5 centimeters extra

.5 liter vinegar

1 teaspoon sugar

juice of one lemon

ESCABECHE
Page 143

.9 kilogram fillet of pike, grouper, swordfish, halibut,
or any other firm white fish

3 tablespoons oil

1 tablespoon vinegar

1 teaspoon salt

$\frac{1}{8}$ teaspoon cayenne pepper

5 centimeter by 2.5 centimeter orange peel, thin, if possible, and without the
white pulp, cut into 2.5 centimeter pieces
resembling shredded coconut

1 teaspoon onion juice or 2 teaspoons grated onion

2 whole fresh bay leaves, washed and broken into 4 or 5 pieces

sprig of fresh thyme or ¼ teaspoon dry thyme

.25 liter very thin slices green pepper (bell pepper, cubinello, or
sweet banana pepper)

1 large orange, peeled and sliced crosswise

4 to 6 large lettuce leaves

TOMATO CURRY
Page 145

1 large can peeled, whole tomatoes
1 teaspoon sugar
½ teaspoon salt
1 tablespoon curry powder
⅛ teaspoon cayenne pepper
.25 liter uncooked, washed Louisiana rice
.25 liter white bread crumbs
4 tablespoons butter (½ stick)
1 tablespoon chopped fresh parsley

JUMBALLAYA A LA CREOLE
Page 147

.25 liter rice
.25 liter water
2 ¾ teaspoons salt
1 chicken, 1 to 1.1 kilograms, cut into 8 pieces
6 tablespoons flour
¾ teaspoon black pepper
1 tablespoon minced or grated onion
4 tablespoons oil
1 bay leaf
1 small can broken tomato pieces
or
1 small can whole tomatoes
½ teaspoon Tabasco sauce
½ teaspoon plus 1 tablespoon sugar
⅛ teaspoon garlic salt

174

4 tablespoons butter (½ stick)

2 tablespoons oil

1 can okra, drained and rinsed

.25 liter frozen peas

1 small can minced clams

.2 kilograms Italian sausage
or
.2 kilograms breakfast sausage

4 to 6 tablespoons parsley, coarsely chopped

NINE-DAY PICKLES
Page 151

INGREDIENTS FOR BRINE:

3.8 liters water

.5 liter salt

3.2 kilograms cucumbers

.9 liter vinegar

1 tablespoon alum (available from pharmacist)

INGREDIENTS FOR SYRUP:

1.4 liters vinegar

1.6 kilograms sugar plus .5 liter

4 tablespoons allspice

2 tablespoons celery seeds

4 cinnamon sticks, 6 to 8 centimeters, each

GIRL SCOUT DRUMSTICKS
Page 153

454 grams ground beef
2 ice cubes, crushed
2 tablespoons chopped onion
½ teaspoon salt
light sprinkling black pepper
1 egg
.25 liter cornflakes

BEEFSTEAK AND BANANAS
Page 155

6 to 8 firm, not-too-ripe bananas
4 teaspoons sugar
1 teaspoon butter
1 teaspoon lemon juice
8 top sirloin steaks, 340 grams each
1 teaspoon salt mixed with ½ teaspoon black pepper
⅛ teaspoon garlic salt
⅛ teaspoon paprika
1 tablespoon Kitchen Bouquet
4 tablespoons shortening (½ butter and ½ oil, or ½ lard and ½ oil)
parsley for garnish

Cookbooks

The following cookbooks were used as sources for the adapted recipes that appear in *American Gastronomy*.

1. *A Collection of Choice Recipes*

   Contributed by the Ladies of Des Moines

2. *Capitol City Cook Book*

   By the Grace Church Woman's Guild

3. *Choice Recipes by Moscow Women*

   Compiled by the Hospitality Committee of the Presbyterian

   Ladies' Aid

4. *Cooking in Old Creole Days*

   By Celestine Eustis

5.   *Dorcas Cook Book*

   Published by the Dorcas Society of St. John Lutheran Church

6.   *Directions for Cookery; in Its Various Branches*

   By Miss Leslie

7.   *Electric Refrigerator Recipes & Menus*

   By Miss Alice Bradley

8.   *Favorite Recipes of Colfax County Club Women*

   By Colfax County Club Women

9.   *Florida Salads*

   By Francis Barber Harris

10.   *Hand-Book of Practical Cookery for Ladies and Professional*
    Cooks

   By Pierre Blot

11.   *High Living: Recipes from Southern Climes*

   By L.L. McLaren

12.   *Home Cookery: A Collection of Tested Receipts*

   By Mrs. Chadwick

13.   *Library Ann's Cook Book*

   Compiled by the Minneapolis Library Staff Association

14.   *Mrs. Porter's New Southern Cookery Book*

   By Mrs. Porter

15. *One Hundred Recipes for the Chafing Dish*

      By H.M. Kinsley

16. *Patriotic Food Show Official Recipe Book*

      By the Women's Central Committee on Food Conservation

17. *Presbyterian Cook Book*

      Compiled by the Ladies of the First Presbyterian Church,

            Dayton, Ohio

18. *Priscilla Cook Book*

      Compiled by the Christian Church Priscilla Aid

19. *The Garfield Women's Club Cook Book*

      By the Garfield Women's Club

20. *The Indian Cook Book*

      By the Indian Women's Club

21. *The Improved Housewife; or Book of Receipts*

      By A Married Lady

22. *The Junior League of Dallas Cook Book*

      Compiled by the Association of Junior Leagues of America

23. *The Kansas Home Cook-Book*

      Compiled by Cushing and Gray

24. *The New Family Book; or Ladies' Indispensable Companion*

      By E. Hutchinson

25.   *Six Little Cooks; or Aunt Jane's Cooking Class*

      By Elizabeth Stansbury Kirkland

26.   *Y.M.C.A. Cook Book*

      Compiled by the Young Men's Christian Association

Index to Recipes

Appleade, 135

Apple Catsup,109

Baked Stuffed Potatoes, 111

Beefsteak and Bananas, 155

Boiled Fowl, 83

Burnt Sugar Cake, 121

Butterscotch Cake Pudding, 115

Chili, 113

Cold Compote, 137

Dresden Dressing, 79

Escabeche, 143

Girl Scout Drumsticks, 153

Grapefruit and Lobster Salad, 95

Ham and Sweet Potato Salad, 91

Hashed Little Neck Clams on Toast, 85

Jumballaya à la Creole, 147

Kitchen Pepper, 127

Mexican Eggs, 77

Mississippi Corn Bread, 75

Nine-Day Pickles, 151

Orange Fool, 129

Oyster Shortcake, 97

Peach Sauce, 73

Peanut Brittle Dessert, 101

Pickled Chicken, 141

Potato Dressing, 93

Round Steak Sausage Forcemeat, 105

Sausages, 69

Stewed Frog Legs, 63

Sweet Potato Buns, 89

Sweet Potato Pudding, 67

Sweet Potato Waffles, 87

Togus Bread, 133

Tomato Curry, 145

Tomato Marmalade, 103

To Fricasee a Small Chicken, Southern Mode, 57

To Pot Cheese, 123

Veal Loaf, 139

Wild Onions and Eggs, 119

Wild Plum Catsup, 131

Wonders or Crullers, 61

Other books by Chef Louis Szathmáry

The Chef's Secret Cook Book, Quadrangle, 1971.

COOKERY AMERICANA
AN ARNO PRESS COLLECTION

Each of the following titles includes an Introduction and Revised Recipes by Chef Louis Szathmáry.

Along the Northern Border: Cookery in Idaho, Minnesota, and North Dakota. New York, 1973.

Cooking in Old Creole Days by Celestine Eustis. New York, 1904.

Cool, Chill, and Freeze: A New Approach to Cookery. New York, 1973.

Directions for Cookery, in Its Various Branches by Miss Eliza Leslie. 31st edition. Philadelphia, 1848.

Fifty Years of Prairie Cooking. New York, 1973.

Hand-Book of Practical Cookery by Pierre Blot. New York, 1869.

High Living: Recipes from Southern Climes. Compiled by L. L. McLaren. San Francisco, 1904.

Home Cookery & Ladies' Indispensable Companion: Cookery in Northeastern Cities. New York, 1973.

The Improved Housewife, or Book of Receipts by Mrs. A. L. Webster. 6th edition. Hartford, 1845.

The Kansas Home Cook-Book. Compiled by Mrs. C. H. Cushing and Mrs. B. Gray. 5th edition. Leavenworth, Kansas, 1886.

Midwestern Home Cookery. New York, 1973.

Mrs. Porter's New Southern Cookery Book by Mrs. M. E. Porter. Philadelphia, 1871.

One Hundred Recipes for the Chafing Dish by H. M. Kinsley. New York, 1894.

Six Little Cooks by Elizabeth Stansbury Kirkland. Chicago, 1879.

Southwestern Cookery: Indian and Spanish Influences. New York, 1973.